THE SHOTS ARE BACK!

THE ALDERSHOT NEWS GROUP

at heart ♡ publications
www.atheart.co.uk

First published in 2008 by
At Heart Ltd
32 Stamford Street
Altrincham
Cheshire
WA14 1EY

in conjunction with
Aldershot News Group
35-39 High Street
Aldershot
Hampshire
GU11 1BH

Compiled by Charlie Oliver

Foreword by Nikki Bull

Match reports by Charlie Oliver, Guy Butchers and Lee Hacker. With thanks to Chris Harris, Marcus Mabberley and Graham Brookland.

News items by Charlie Oliver. With thanks to Chris Harris and Rob Kelly.

Photographs by Chris Whiteoak, Alistair Wilson and Steve Porter. With thanks to Ben White.

Statistics with thanks to Pete Stanford.

ISBN: 978-1-84547-216-0

Printed and bound by Ashford Colour Press, Gosport

CONTENTS

FOREWORD

Exeter, 15 April 2008: a date that I shall never forget. Its cherished memories will go with me to the grave. A night when a dream became reality, when the phoenix finally rose from the ashes.

After 16 years, the people of Aldershot once again had a Football League club to support. More importantly, the club had completed the journey back to where Aldershot football belongs.

Having been at the club for six years, I know how much hard work the supporters of Aldershot have devoted to get their club up and running again after it was so cruelly taken away from them in 1992.

Hundreds have dedicated their lives to Aldershot Town and the rebirth of Aldershot football. That April evening was their moment, when all their efforts were finally rewarded, and I felt truly privileged to have been at St James Park that night and to be part of those celebrations. Our success was built by a united club, from chairman, John McGinty, down to Lisa, the tea lady. Everyone has been pulling in the same direction from Day One.

It was, and is, a real joy being part of this squad. I cannot underestimate the power of a united dressing room and a true team spirit. At the start of pre-season, not a pundit anywhere in the land gave us a mention in their Conference promotion predictions, and to be honest, who could blame them? I can think of at least eight teams that appeared to have stronger credentials than us on paper.

But whatever we may have lacked in experience and recognisable players, we more than made up for in work ethic and a sheer will to win. As a team, and as friends, there was nothing we would not have done for each other this year, and we took that spirit onto the pitch with us. It's no coincidence that we managed to win so many games when not playing at our very best and a staggering 21 of our 31 wins were achieved by a one-goal margin.

It is hard to single out any one memory from so many great ones, but Scott Davies' 95th-minute winner at Torquay in early March was our season's defining moment and the goal that our fans will remember more than any other. We withstood Torquay's second-half onslaught, and stole the three points at the death. I think that result knocked the stuffing out of Torquay; the title race was firmly in our hands and we never looked back.

Losing to eventual winners Ebbsfleet United in the FA Trophy semi-final was the only disappointment in a wonderful season, tempered a little by our victory in the Setanta Shield. Every player dreams of running out at Wembley, and every supporter would love the chance to sing their songs at 'the home of football'. But over the two legs against Ebbsfleet we had no complaints.

But in my mind the Trophy final is actually only a day out, albeit a very good one. Promotion, however, is life-changing, and that was the mission given to us by Gary Waddock and Martin Kuhl on the first day of pre-season. I wouldn't swap winning the league for anything in the world.

On a personal level, the club and its supporters have given me so much affection and support in my six years here that I knew the only way I could ever come close to repaying them was to be part of the squad that took Aldershot football back into the Football League. To have done so is wonderful.

It goes to show that dreams really do come true.

Nikki Bull

Nikki Bull is the current Aldershot Town goalkeeper. The 26-year-old joined the club in 2002 and has made 278 appearances (before the start of the 2008/09 season). He started all but two of Aldershot's Blue Square Premier championship-winning 2007/08 season and was voted both the players' and the fans' Player of the Year.

March 25, 1992: The day the football died.

On that woeful Wednesday Aldershot FC was wound up in the High Court and their results were expunged from season 1991/92. A trip to Cardiff City, five days before, was the club's last ever fixture.

While Football League Division Four had lost a replaceable member, the town of Aldershot and its football following had lost its soul. After 66 years the Shots, members of the Football League since 1932, were shot.

But a few Shots fans had other ideas. Terry Owens and Graham Brookland, less than a month after the demise of Aldershot FC, announced that they had formed Aldershot Town Football Club (1992).

It was April 22, 1992, three days after Easter, and this was a resurrection, with the new club's 'phoenix from the ashes' badge reflecting unbreakable ties with the old Aldershot FC. Two guises add up to one body: the Shots. Senior status was granted and the Diadora (Isthmian) League welcomed Aldershot Town FC into their Division Three for season 1992/93.

Under manager Steve Wignall – a former Aldershot FC player – the Shots, with Mark Butler's goals to the fore, romped to successive promotions, backed by fans in their thousands, even away from home. The Isthmian League had seen nothing like it. Football and Aldershot were together again, and better, perhaps, than ever before.

In 1998, under the colourful management of George Borg, the club won promotion to the Isthmian Premier and, with Gary Abbott taking on Butler's goal-scoring mantle, the Hampshire Senior Cup took up near-permanent residence at the Rec, thanks to wins in 1999, 2000, 2002 and 2003.

But the Shots had higher ambitions: a return to the Football League. Under Terry Brown's inspirational leadership, the Isthmian championship was secured in season 2002/03 and with it promotion to the Nationwide Conference. The Shots were back on the national stage, just one division away from their old home in the Football League. Twice, only penalties denied Brown and his Shots that coveted promotion, in the 2004 and 2005 play-offs.

By that game in 2005, Aldershot Town had gone professional, but it was not until the arrival of manager Gary Waddock and his professionalism, in the summer of 2007, that the phoenix finally roosted in the Football League.

This is the story of how Waddock and his assistant, Martin Kuhl, masterminded the unexpectedly wondrous season of 2007/08, when the Shots romped to the Conference title, securing the Setanta Shield to boot, playing fabulous football along the way.

'April is the cruellest month' wrote T.S. Eliot in 'The Waste Land', but not so for Aldershot Town. Sixteen years after that day in April 1992 when hope sprung eternal, promotion was secured at Exeter City on another April day, sparking jubilant scenes as the Aldershot family – fans, players and management – danced together on the terraces. One of football's greatest and most emotional comebacks had been achieved.

Talking of wastelands, some regard non-League football as such, but Aldershot fans will tell you that it is a wonderful place, full of thrills and spills. But it's onwards and upwards for those fans. They are back in the land of plenty, the Football League. And it is their burning desire that has fuelled the phoenix's fire.

So, while Waddock and his squad are now busy making sure they make their mark in League Two, sit back and revel in their triumphant march there, in what was the greatest season in the history of Aldershot football.

Charlie Oliver
Sports Editor, *Aldershot News & Mail*

PRE-SEASON

18 May 2007
WADDOCK RUMOURED TO BE THE NEW SHOTS MANAGER

After eight weeks of searching, Aldershot are finally set to unveil former QPR boss Gary Waddock as their new manager.

As the News went to press, the 45-year-old had yet to be confirmed as Terry Brown's successor but it is believed that an appointment will be made within days after he held off the challenge of caretaker manager Martin Kuhl.

The Aldershot board interviewed eight candidates for the vacant manager's position on May 3, before cutting that shortlist down to just three names – thought to be Waddock, Kuhl and former Gillingham boss Andy Hessenthaler.

It is believed that it came down to a straight fight between Waddock and Kuhl, with the former QPR man attracting enough support from the board for an appointment to be made imminently.

Waddock told the News earlier this week that he is looking to get back into football as soon as possible, but refused to confirm or deny that he had been in talks with Aldershot.

However, despite being reluctant to admit his interest in the post, Waddock is expected to take the reins at the Rec and is likely to keep Kuhl on the payroll.

The former Republic of Ireland international enjoyed an impressive playing career, making 203 appearances for QPR over eight years before leaving for a two-year spell at Belgian club Charleroi in 1987.

He returned to English football in 1989 with Millwall, before going back for a second period at QPR, followed by spells at Swindon Town, Bristol Rovers and Luton Town before retiring.

Waddock soon moved on to the coaching staff at Loftus Road after being given a job with the QPR youth academy and, following Ian Holloway's suspension in February 2006, he was appointed caretaker manager, helping Rangers to avoid relegation.

22 May 2007
WADDOCK ARRIVES

Aldershot have appointed former QPR boss Gary Waddock as their new manager after he held off competition from more than 30 candidates to secure the post.

The 45-year-old has signed a two-year contract at the Rec and assumes overall responsibility for first team, reserve and youth team affairs. He is responsible for all football-related budgets and will provide guidance for the junior section as well.

It has also been confirmed that caretaker manager Martin Kuhl will stay at the club, reverting to his role as first team coach.

"I am absolutely delighted to have got the job," Waddock said. "I am really looking forward to the challenge of taking this club forward and it is a great opportunity for me.

"Martin and I will be working hard this summer to make sure we're ready for the new season and we have been in close contact already. This is a good, well-run club and I'm really looking forward to getting started."

"We are delighted that Gary has agreed to join as manager," said Aldershot chairman John McGinty (pictured above right). "Gary was impressive in interview and his enthusiasm for the job shone through, with an obvious desire to succeed.

"He has extensive experience in developing young players and we believe that is a vital ingredient to our future."

25 May 2007
WADDOCK HAS BIG PLANS FOR ALDERSHOT TOWN

New Aldershot manager Gary Waddock has insisted that he is aiming for long-term progression rather than instant progression – with promotion to League One the ultimate aim.

"Everybody would like promotion to the Football League in my first year as manager and expectation is very high at this football club. Obviously I would like promotion straight away too but, personally, I would rather a period of success over three, four or five years. Yes, we want

Football League status but we don't just want to get this club into League Two, but maybe a league higher than that.

"There's a good base of players at this club already. Come pre-season we will have a group of players here who we hope will have the same hunger and desire for success as me and Martin [Kuhl].

"Martin Kuhl is a talented coach and we will be a good partnership. It's a good combination to have, and with his experience at Conference level he will be a big asset to me.

"I have a real hunger and desire to succeed and I want to take this club forward. I'm an experienced coach and I like working with players on a day-to-day basis. I'm going to need the players and everyone at the club to be pulling in the same direction, and if we can do that then we have a good chance of success.

"We're going to be a good footballing side but at times we are going to have to mix it up. But I like my teams to pass the ball and play good football."

Waddock has begun his Aldershot revolution by allowing 35-year-old left-back Darren Barnard, the former Chelsea player, to leave the club. "It was a difficult decision for me and everyone at the club to let Darren go but we are looking to the future."

3 July 2007
SHOTS SQUAD
TAKES SHAPE

Aldershot manager Gary Waddock has admitted he is delighted with the way his squad is shaping up for the new season – and revealed that more new faces are expected to arrive imminently.

The former QPR boss made his first forays into the transfer market last week to land Altrincham midfielder Lewis Chalmers and WBA striker Rob Elvins on free transfers, and he now has his sights firmly set on securing further additions within the coming weeks.

The former Republic of Ireland international hopes to bring in four top class players to complement his talented squad, and told the Mail that he has been pleased with developments so far.

"It is a complicated process but we are making progress and I would hope that within the next couple of weeks we will have the squad fully in place," he said.

"I am really pleased to have brought both Rob (Elvins) and Lewis (Chalmers) to the club because they're both quality players.

"Rob is from West Brom and is a very talented forward, while Lewis is a current England National Game XI player.

"I have no complaints on the transfer front so far – they are both young, quality players who will really add something to the squad and both were my number one targets."

It is thought that the Shots are hoping to land a left-back to replace Darren Barnard, another two midfielders and a pacy centre half, with Anthony Charles possibly in line for a permanent move to the Rec after a successful loan spell at the end of last season.

10 July 2007
BULL STAYS ON
AT ALDERSHOT

Aldershot boss Gary Waddock has been handed a major boost after Nikki Bull committed his future to the club for the forthcoming season.

The 25-year-old is arguably the best keeper outside of the Football League and has been linked with a host of clubs this summer, including Brentford, Millwall and Brighton & Hove Albion.

"There has been a lot of speculation and rumours over the past few weeks and I thought that it was the right

time to put all that to an end," said Bull.

"I have had several meetings with the manager and chairman and I have a year left on my contract and I am here to stay.

"I was frustrated last season because I really care about this club and we have to do much better this time around. It should be an exciting season but we need to deliver once a week and not just once a month or so."

Waddock was delighted to have kept his keeper. "I rate Nikki very highly. I know he wants to play at a higher level but hopefully he can achieve that here with us. It is such a boost that he is staying. You don't want to lose your best players."

WILLIAMS INJURY IS 'MASSIVE BLOW' FOR THE SHOTS

Aldershot boss Gary Waddock has admitted that losing winger Ryan Williams for the start of the season is a 'massive blow'.

The former Bristol Rovers midfielder sustained a serious knee injury in last Tuesday night's friendly against Crystal Palace and it has been confirmed that he has partially torn the anterior cruciate ligament in his left leg.

Waddock told the Mail that even in the best case scenario the 28-year-old will not be back to full fitness for at least two months. "It is a massive blow. He scored 14 goals from the wings last season and to try to replace him is a big problem. We have to find 14 goals from somewhere else in the team.

"The whole left side needs replacing and you cannot just pluck players out of the sky, so there is a lot of work ahead."

Williams was eventually ruled out for nine months, returning in April 2008 to start just one league match in the 2007/08 season.

7 August 2007
WADDOCK NAMES DAY AS CAPTAIN

Gary Waddock has named central defender Rhys Day as his captain for the coming season.

Waddock believes he has picked a real leader as his team prepare for the assault on the Blue Square Premier.

"I looked around the group during pre-season and I have seen his leadership qualities.

"He has a tremendous amount of respect in the dressing room and he has all the qualities needed to do a great job for us. To back that up he is a top-quality player too."

10 August 2007
GRANT IS READY TO TAKE ON LEAGUE FAVOURITES

Shots striker John Grant believes the first few months of the season will be vital if the team are to realise any promotion ambitions.

"We want to get off to a good start, which will give us a platform to build on for the rest of the year.

"The first few games can dictate how the whole season unfolds. Winning the first few games has to be the aim, so we don't get left behind.

"We want to be successful and we want to be in and around the top ten when we come to the run-in, so a fast start is important."

Grant revealed that he is relishing the chance of taking on some of the promotion favourites early in the season, with the likes of Torquay United, Oxford United, Exeter City and York City on the fixture list in the first two months.

"Everyone knows who the big guns are and who will be up there when the end of the season comes. It's a good opportunity to play them so soon and I'm looking forward to it. You have to do well against those sides if you are going to challenge in this league."

Grant was last season's top scorer and also won the supporters' player of the season award. But he refuses to set himself a goal target.

"I don't say to myself that I need to have scored 20 goals by Christmas or anything like that. Every game I go into I want to score and I believe in my ability. That is my target."

Grant is happy with the way things have looked in pre-season. "We have had to knuckle down but overall things have gone well for us. It has left us in a good position but we don't want to get carried away. Last summer pre-season went quite well and then we didn't do ourselves justice in the league.

"The real hard work starts on Saturday, when we go to Kidderminster."

—————— 10 August 2007
WADDOCK'S MEN ARE 'READY TO TAKE ON ANYONE'

Gary Waddock feels his squad is ready for what will be another highly competitive Conference season.

"I am happy with what I have got in the squad," said the manager, who took over at Aldershot Town in May.

This week Waddock brought in defenders Rob Gier and Anthony Straker, brought midfielder Ben Harding back to the Recreation Ground and also signed Venezuelan goalkeeper Mikhael Jaimez-Ruiz as cover for Nikki Bull.

"There is now healthy competition in all areas of the pitch, which can only be a good thing. That's all you can ask for when you are going into a new season.

"The competition means that nobody can take their foot off the pedal at any point. If they are not performing, the players all know there is someone waiting behind them to grab their chance."

Although confident in his new look squad's ability, Waddock refuses to reveal what his target is for the new season.

"It will depend on the start we make and we are looking to pick up points as quickly as possible. I don't want to go shouting about how we are going to do and where we're going to go, but we are confident we can do well.

"The group of players we have are fit and ready to take on anyone in this league. I think Stevenage, Torquay, Rushden & Diamonds and Exeter will all be strong, and probably a few others too.

"But the other managers will all be looking around and saying the same thing as me. It's going to be a closely fought league."

KIDDERMINSTER HARRIERS 1

(Creighton 77)

ALDERSHOT TOWN 2

(Davies 46, John Grant 58)

11 August 2007

LINE-UP
Bull, Smith, Straker, Day, Charles, Harding, Soares, Chalmers (Hudson 66), Davies, John Grant, Elvins.

Aldershot manager Gary Waddock made the perfect start to his reign with three points away to much-fancied Kidderminster Harriers on Saturday.

It was a result built on a mix of hard work, fitness, youthful enthusiasm and clinical finishing.

Midfielder Scott Davies and John Grant sealed the victory with second-half strikes, and although Harriers pulled a goal back, the Shots held on.

Kidderminster were the slightly better side in the first half and did miss two gilt-edged chances, but overall the Shots were good value for their win.

In the eighth minute, Harriers' striker James Constable intercepted an underhit back pass and rounded Nikki Bull, but shot into the side netting from six yards.

But Aldershot were making chances of their own, and they looked particularly effective with set pieces. A 20th-minute header from Rhys Day went the wrong side of the left-hand upright, while four minutes later a 25-yard free kick from Davies thundered inches wide of the same post.

When a team doesn't take chances like those squandered by Kidderminster, they usually pay for it and accordingly it took the Shots just seven seconds in the second half to break the deadlock.

Straight from the kick-off, 19-year-old Davies, on a season's loan from Reading, ran unchallenged at the heart of the Kidderminster defence. He unleashed a thunderous drive from 20 yards that flew into the back

of the net, prompting Davies to celebrate with the 413 travelling Aldershot fans.

> " *I don't score many goals, so my celebration was a bit wild. Gary Waddock told me the aim was for promotion and this is likely to be one of the hardest away trips.* "
>
> Scott Davies

Davies turned creator for the Shots' second goal when, making ground down the right-hand touchline, he delivered a well-hit low cross to Rob Elvins who turned and shot from eight yards. Giant goalkeeper Scott Bevan saved well, but was unable to hold on to the ball and John Grant was on hand to knock it home from a yard out to send the travelling fans into ecstasy behind the goal.

It was inevitable that there would be a backlash from the home side, and the introduction of powerhouse striker Iyseden Christie on 67 minutes proved the catalyst, adding a bit of spark and energy to Kidderminster's forward play.

The home side pulled a goal back on 77 minutes when centre-half Mark Creighton met a corner with precision timing to send it rocketing home from ten yards. Bull had

© Kidderminster Shuttle

Lewis Chalmers battles for possession.

absolutely no chance as the header flashed past him.

There was plenty of Kidderminster possession in the last 15 minutes but it was dealt with in a calm and efficient manner by the Shots.

The only downside was picking up six bookings, but that was more to do with over-enthusiasm and fussiness from the referee than anything sinister.

The Aldershot defence kept its line well and in particular the young full-backs Dean Smith and Anthony Straker showed a good deal of promise. And Day and Anthony Charles appear to have the makings of a decent pairing in the centre, with very little getting past them in the air.

> " It was a great performance. We were very professional, which was pleasing. We are happy as we obviously would have taken a win at the start of the game. I think we defended brilliantly all game and especially after they scored. We looked really threatening on the break too. "
>
> Gary Waddock

ALDERSHOT TOWN 0

15 August 2007

TORQUAY UNITED 3

(Sills 6, Stevens 45, Zebroski 56)

LINE-UP

Bull, Gier (Hudson 53), Straker, Day, Charles, Davies, Soares, Chalmers, John Grant, Elvins, Harding.

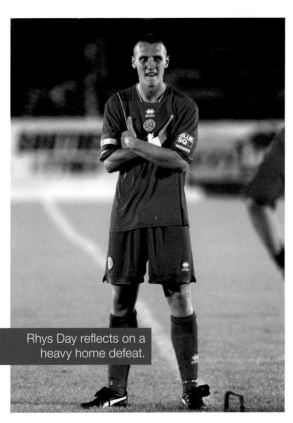

Rhys Day reflects on a heavy home defeat.

Indeed, only a string of fine saves from Bull stopped Sills from adding to Aldershot's misery. Torquay were strong and committed and dominated play, even if the Shots did come back strongly later in the half.

Rob Elvins and Rhys Day both missed opportunities, but John Grant missed the best of them, blocked by the legs of Torquay keeper Simon Rayner.

Elvins came close again to equalising but instead, the Shots went in 2-0 down, when substitute Danny Stevens, who had just come on for Tony Bedeau, waltzed into the area and gave Bull no chance with a fine finish.

Torquay were confident and composed in the second half with their two-goal cushion, and Chris Zebroski killed off the Shots with a close-range header.

Bull remained outstanding, making super saves from Lee Phillips and Kevin Nicholson, in what was a rude awakening for the rest of the Shots.

Aldershot were brought crashing back to earth with a 3-0 defeat at home by promotion rivals Torquay United, who were making their first away trip outside of the Football League since 1927.

The Shots were often outclassed by the visiting Gulls, who created a succession of early opportunities.

They took the lead inside the first ten minutes when Scott Davies lost possession in the middle and the ball reached former Shot, Tim Sills. His placed effort was deflected past Nikki Bull, who had no chance with the goal. Sills did not celebrate against his former team.

> **" I don't get carried away and I'm not too disappointed tonight. You have to stay calm. We would have loved to have won but we haven't and we have got to show some courage. Mistakes have cost us dearly. We created chances but didn't take them and we got punished. Torquay did not disappoint, they'll be up there come the end of the season. "**
>
> Gary Waddock

18 August 2007

ALDERSHOT TOWN 3
(John Grant 58, Chalmers 67, Harding 82)

DROYLSDEN 1
(Fearns 25)

Aldershot bounced back from their midweek disappointment against Torquay, convincingly defeating Blue Square Premier new boys Droylsden and giving boss Gary Waddock his first home win in charge.

Even at this early stage of the season there had been talk of pressure on Waddock, but his young team made sure that there were no grumbles from the Shots faithful with a dominant second-half display.

Starting with the same line-up that had been soundly beaten by Torquay the previous Wednesday, the Shots indeed kicked off looking like a side that had been beaten 3-0 just three days earlier.

Edgy and tense from the off, it was often Droylsden who looked the more aggressive and hungry.

Aldershot did have an opportunity after 14 minutes when John Grant played in his strike partner Rob Elvins, but Paul Phillips rushed out of the Droylsden goal to smother Elvins' effort.

After 21 minutes, Droylsden fired a warning shot to their hosts when Jamie McGuire cut inside from the left and unleashed a fierce drive that sailed just wide of Nikki Bull's left post. The warning went unheeded as four minutes later the visitors were ahead. A long ball forward by Droylsden full-back Robert Marsh-Evans found Terry Fearns, who out-muscled his marker and powered his way through to lift the ball over the stranded Bull.

John Grant did miss a good chance to find parity just before the break but missed the target and Waddock, clearly unhappy, sent his players out early for the second half, bringing on Kirk Hudson and Jonny Dixon for Louie Soares and Rob Elvins.

The changes worked immediately, with Aldershot looking far more pacy and dynamic.

Ben Harding began to create, drifting in from the left wing, and after 52 minutes the former MK Dons man might have opened his Aldershot account with a stinging drive, but it was well-saved low down by Phillips.

Just before the hour mark Aldershot were level. After a scramble in the Droylsden area, Anthony Charles found himself in unfamiliar territory on the right and crossed for Grant to volley home.

John Grant races Droylsden's Colin Cryan for the ball.

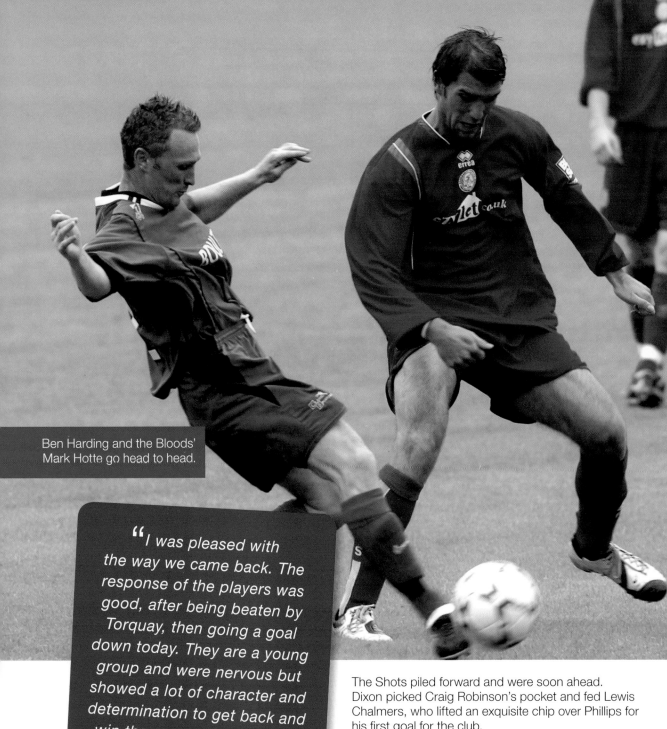

Ben Harding and the Bloods' Mark Hotte go head to head.

> **"** I was pleased with the way we came back. The response of the players was good, after being beaten by Torquay, then going a goal down today. They are a young group and were nervous but showed a lot of character and determination to get back and win the game. I can't repeat what I said to them at half time, but they responded. We've got six out of nine points, which isn't a bad start. **"**
>
> Gary Waddock

The Shots piled forward and were soon ahead. Dixon picked Craig Robinson's pocket and fed Lewis Chalmers, who lifted an exquisite chip over Phillips for his first goal for the club.

After that it was plain sailing for the home side, although there was still enough time for Ben Harding to score his first goal for the Shots. After getting to the byline, Anthony Straker produced a perfect cross, which Harding volleyed home powerfully.

24 August 2007

HISTON 1
(Akurang 65)

ALDERSHOT TOWN 2
(Davies 31, 39)

Sharp-shooting Scott Davies fired his side to their third win in four games and challenged his Aldershot teammates to mount a serious promotion challenge.

The on-loan Reading teenager is fast gaining a reputation for scoring spectacular goals, and he didn't disappoint against Histon, with a bullet 35-yard free kick.

"I've scored three this season and I don't usually score much," Davies said. "The wall was a bit to the left and they left the near post open so I thought, if I just strike it as hard as I can, I might get lucky. We didn't expect to get off to such a flying start. We set a target to get promotion and I don't think it's beyond us."

Aldershot started slowly and gave their hosts a number of opportunities early on in the game. After just two minutes, Histon's Erkan Okay whipped in a cross from the left that was poked just wide by ex-Aldershot striker Cliff Akurang.

The big forward was a constant menace for the Shots' defence early on and after ten minutes he left Anthony Charles for dead wide on the left. But after neatly cutting inside, Akurang's shot was deflected wide.

On 15 minutes, Rhys Day rose well at the far post to meet a deep Davies free kick, but the skipper's header hit the bar and dropped into the arms of the grateful Histon goalkeeper Mark Osborn. The chance sparked Aldershot into life and their young midfield grew in confidence, but with the Histon defence standing firm, something special was needed to break the deadlock.

After 31 minutes, Davies delivered when Lewis Chalmers was brought down 35 yards from goal. Davies had only one thing on his mind: unleashing a rocket shot that flew into the goal past the helpless Osborn.

Eight minutes later it was two when Davies' deflected shot from the edge of the area wrong-footed the Histon keeper.

Aldershot continued their dominance in the second half with Harding, Grant and Straker all going close.

Rhys Day wins a header as Ben Harding shouts encouragement.

© Cambridge Evening News

"In the second half we knew they were going to come out chucking the kitchen sink at us and that's what they did."

Scott Davies

Histon pulled a goal back on 65 minutes when Nikki Bull failed to hold a corner and Akurang turned the ball home. Despite the Shots' protests, the goal was given and Histon laid siege to the Aldershot goal.

With 12 minutes to go, Bull made up for his error when he made an acrobatic save to tip Nathaniel Knight-Percival's header over the bar. Despite the pressure, Aldershot held on to maintain their 100 per cent away record.

Boss Waddock said: "In the second half we didn't play as well. We knew Histon were going to come after us and put us on the back foot, but the pleasing thing for me is that we held out with a young group of players."

ALDERSHOT TOWN 0

CRAWLEY TOWN 1

(Pittman 53)

LINE-UP

Bull, Gier (Soares 71), Straker, Day, Charles, Chalmers, Hudson, Davies, John Grant, Dixon, Harding.

After slumping to a second disappointing home defeat of the season, Aldershot boss Gary Waddock admitted that defensive slip-ups are costing his side.

Aldershot dominated the play against Crawley, hitting the woodwork three times and wasting a host of opportunities, but it was defensive lapses that worried Waddock.

"Keeping clean sheets is something that we haven't done, and that's one thing that I spoke to the players about after today's game," Waddock said.

> **" I couldn't have asked any more of the players. They gave it their all. "**

"We played very well. We hit the woodwork a few times and their goalkeeper made a number of good saves, but we ended up with nothing."

It wasn't for want of trying that Aldershot slipped up against Crawley.

Dominating the match from the off, the Shots could have taken the lead after just two minutes when Ashley Bayes saved well from John Grant after being put through by Ben Harding. Anthony Charles and Grant then flashed headers just wide.

Half time arrived after more good opportunities for Anthony Straker, Jonny Dixon and Charles, but the Shots just could not find a way through.

Jon-Paul Pittman celebrates.

Anthony Charles rues a missed chance.

Then, seven minutes into the second half, the Recreation Ground was stunned into silence when an unmarked Jon-Paul Pittman headed in Dannie Bulman's free kick. The silence was short-lived, however, as Pittman's over-exuberant celebrations drew the wrath of the North Bank, and the referee, who booked the striker for his troubles.

The booking provoked an angry response from the often vocal Crawley manager Steve Evans, who was reprimanded by the referee after clashing with Aldershot assistant Martin Kuhl.

After 56 minutes, a trademark Scott Davies free kick was brilliantly tipped on to the post by the Crawley keeper. Just a minute later, Davies played in Jonny Dixon who had his shot charged down by Bayes, who by now was under more fire than an England manager.

In the 67th minute, Aldershot thought they had been gifted a route back into the game when Pittman drew his second yellow card, following a late challenge on Rob Gier. Making the long walk of shame off the pitch, Pittman got a lesson in humility as he again faced the North Bank crowd that he had earlier needlessly mocked.

With 15 minutes left, substitute Louie Soares began a frantic passage of play when his curling shot hit the far post and was cleared. From the resulting corner Rhys Day had a powerful header cleared off the line. Then,

just a minute later, Davies saw his 25-yard drive brilliantly saved by Bayes. Shortly after that Aldershot struck the post again, this time from a Lewis Chalmers header.

Ben Harding also saw a header flash just wide late on, as it became clear that it just was not Aldershot's day.

> "It's our third home game and our second defeat and it's not really good enough. We are disappointed because if we want to be pushing towards the end of the season we need to be winning our home games. We've looked at how many goals we've conceded this season and it's far too many."
>
> Anthony Charles

ALTRINCHAM 1
(Tinson 45)

1 September 2007

ALDERSHOT TOWN 2
(Dixon 24, Soares 78)

Aldershot produced a hard-working, committed display to grab an important victory at Altrincham on Saturday. The narrow win was the Shots' third in as many away games this season and lifted them to fourth in the Blue Square Premier.

It is often said that the sign of a good side is one that can grind out a result when they have not played well, and that was the case for the Shots, who may still play better this season and lose.

This sort of performance has been missing in recent seasons, but the Shots' determination was clear to see on Saturday.

Jonny Dixon curled the Shots ahead midway through the first half, but Nikki Bull's mistake allowed the home side to level.

Louie Soares came up with the winner, but boss Gary Waddock admitted after the game that he had a few stern words to say at the interval.

Waddock decided not to risk talismanic striker John Grant, who pulled a muscle in his back during a circuit training session, so Rob Elvins returned in attack. Soares also returned in place of Kirk Hudson, and veteran Ricky Newman was on the bench after his summer operation.

Altrincham's Chris Senior was at the heart of a bright start by the home side, forcing Bull into a save from his overhead kick and having a volley blocked on the six-yard line. But it was no surprise when a clinical Shots' counter attack put them a goal up on 24 minutes. The energetic Ben Harding surged out of defence and fed Dixon, who cut inside and curled a delightful finish from 20 yards. Harding and Dixon then set up Scott Davies, whose ferocious drive was straight at goalkeeper Stuart Coburn.

Senior remained a threat but the Shots should have gone in 2-0 up, only for Elvins, put clean through by Davies, to place his shot inches on the wrong side of the far post.

Instead, in added time, Rob Gier gave away a free kick and Bull misjudged Steve Aspinall's delivery, palming the ball back from under his bar, for Darren Tinson to blast the ball into the empty net.

It was a rare blunder from Bull, so often the saviour for Aldershot, and he was clearly angry with himself as he kicked his post with fury.

The second half saw the game open up, as both sides looked for the winner. The Shots created a number of openings with Rhys Day, Soares, Lewis Chalmers (playing against his old club), Anthony Charles and Davies all missing chances to put the visitors back in front.

The decisive goal came on 77 minutes. Anthony Straker galloped down the left and passed to Harding. The elegant midfielder picked out Soares at the far post, who slammed the ball home.

The Shots were under pressure for the last ten minutes as Altrincham piled forward, and Bull redeemed himself with a good save from Gareth Whalley's shot to secure yet another win on the road for Waddock's side.

FOREST GREEN ROVERS 2
(Fleetwood 2, Jones 81)

ALDERSHOT TOWN 3
(John Grant 11, 55, Dixon 27)

LINE-UP

Bull, Gier, Straker, Day, Charles, Chalmers, Soares, Davies, John Grant, Dixon (Newman 44), Harding (Winfield 85).

A brilliant display saw Aldershot Town pick up a fourth successive away win, this time at Forest Green Rovers.

Two goals from John Grant and another from Jonny Dixon capped an impressive performance, marred only by a red card for young left-back Anthony Straker.

Shots boss Gary Waddock has instilled great belief in his young squad and this display showed both their attacking and defensive qualities after a first half full of creativity, flowing football, pace and quality. After Straker's dismissal late in the first half, Waddock's side showed that they can battle for a result too, with a mixture of resilience and determination.

The start that Aldershot have made this season has been above the expectations of the supporters, and possibly the players too. Waddock must now make sure the players keep their feet on the ground after this impressive opening.

In truth, however, Waddock's men could not have made a worse start to this game. Nikki Bull denied Stuart Fleetwood, clean through, after just 14 seconds, and the striker made no mistake with a second opportunity only a minute later.

The Shots' record at Forest Green has not been impressive in recent years but Waddock's side maintained their freshness and belief with Dixon going close to an equaliser. And John Grant, back from injury, equalised in the 11th minute, thumping a header home from Louie Soares' cross.

Before the half hour, the Shots had turned the game on its head. Lewis Chalmers crossed from the right, captain Rhys Day made a nuisance of himself, and Dixon forced home the loose ball.

But the game took another twist in the 42nd minute, when Straker ended up on the wrong side of a long ball, clipping Les Afful's heels as he sped towards goal. The inevitable red card forced Waddock into a reshuffle and left Grant on his own up front, with Ricky Newman coming on into midfield.

Ten-man Aldershot needed a great start to the second half, and they got it. After good work from Scott Davies and Chalmers, Grant nodded home another cross from Soares.

Rovers' expected onslaught did come, however, and only Bull's inspired keeping ensured the Shots won the game. Darren Jones finally scored with nine minutes remaining but the Shots held on, with Bull to the fore.

> "This was a tremendous performance, right through the team. We played some great football in the first half and then dug in after the break. We were really sharp in attack and even when we went down to ten men we went and scored the third."
>
> Gary Waddock

ALDERSHOT TOWN 5

(Day 28, Davies 37, 60, John Grant 62, Elvins 90)

NORTHWICH VICTORIA 0

Scott Davies led the charge as Aldershot Town thrashed woeful Northwich Victoria to go top of the Blue Square Premier.

Two goals from the on-loan midfield star, and strikes from captain Rhys Day, striker John Grant and a first for the club from forward Rob Elvins in injury time, capped an impressive display from the Shots, who must now be thinking of a genuine promotion push.

The commitment from the young squad was evident throughout this one-sided affair, with all of the players showing a desire to impress boss Gary Waddock, whose enthusiasm has clearly rubbed off on his team.

The demolition – the Shots' third successive victory – means they have taken 18 points from eight league games.

Northwich were all at sea after defenders Josh Wilson and Michael Welch sustained head injuries early in the first half and had to be replaced.

The Shots took the lead in the 27th minute, when Lewis Chalmers launched a bullet throw into the Vics' penalty box. Day leapt like a salmon to head the ball powerfully into the bottom corner of the net.

It marked the beginning of a torrid afternoon for Vics goalkeeper Ben Connett, who struggled to cope with the peppering that his goal received. That said, Michael Coulson should have equalized straight after Day's goal but pushed a shot wide of Nikki Bull's goalposts.

The scare galvanised Aldershot and the inevitable second goal came in the 37th minute when the impressive Davies took on a pass from Grant and struck a rasping shot into the net from 15 yards.

Davies, fresh from receiving the Blue Square Premier Player of the Month award before the game, slammed home his second of the game and fifth of the season after the break.

Northwich disintegrated as the difference in ability, organisation and skill showed once more two minutes later. A pinpoint cross from Barbados international

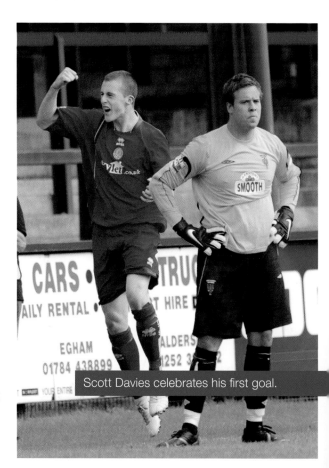

Scott Davies celebrates his first goal.

Rhys Day, after heading Aldershot ahead.

Louie Soares was met by Grant, who nodded home at the far post to notch his fifth goal of the season.

At the other end, Bull made two superb saves from Dino Maamria, helping him keep his first clean sheet of the season.

Elvins' committed display produced the goal he deserved deep into injury time after Connett was judged to have handled a back pass just outside the six-yard box.

With all ten Vics outfield players huddled on the line, substitute Ricky Newman teed up Elvins, who powered a shot along the ground which went underneath the jumping Northwich players.

He was mobbed by his delighted teammates in what was probably relief as much as joy as he bagged his first goal for the club.

Just eight die-hard Vics fans made the trip to the Rec from Cheshire and their journey home must have felt even longer after witnessing this spineless display.

> " It was an excellent result. We wanted to keep a clean sheet because all good sides build from the back with solid foundations. The team spirit was fantastic and you could see that by the reaction to Rob Elvins' goal. Everything is very positive at the moment and it's great to be top of the league because that's where every team wants to be. "
>
> Gary Waddock

OXFORD UNITED 2

(Jeannin 46, Shaw 55)

ALDERSHOT TOWN 3

(John Grant 15 pen, 43, Chalmers 83)

15 September 2007

LINE-UP

Bull, Gier, Straker, Charles (Hudson 65), Winfield, Chalmers, Soares, Davies, Elvins (Newman 79), John Grant, Harding.

Gary Waddock's hot Shots continued their impressive form with an entertaining victory at Oxford United on Saturday, outwitting his former mentor Jim Smith to maintain Aldershot's 100 per cent away record and confirm the Shots as genuine promotion candidates.

"In the first half we were brilliant and second half we dug in and showed great character."

John Grant

Following the 5-0 demolition of Northwich Victoria last week, Waddock made one change, bringing Anthony Straker back into the side, following a one-match ban, in place of the injured captain Rhys Day. New signing Joel Grant was on the bench.

With Anthony Charles returning from left-back alongside David Winfield, it was a new pairing at centre-back for the Shots that would be rarely troubled in the first half at the Kassam Stadium.

In front of a vocal travelling army of 900 Aldershot supporters, neither side managed to stamp their authority on a scrappy opening period. With both midfields cancelling each other out it took a moment of madness from Oxford defender Arthur Gnohere to open up the game.

After 14 minutes the Frenchman chose to punch, rather than head away a Scott Davies corner, giving the referee little option than to award a penalty. It was left to John Grant, who with three goals in his previous two matches, strode up confidently, sending Billy Turley in the Oxford goal the wrong way. Ten minutes later, Grant might have doubled the lead when his flick from a Straker cross was directed straight at the Oxford goalkeeper.

With the Shots well on top, the home side took 42

minutes to create their first opportunity when Marvin Robinson's run from deep evaded the Aldershot offside trap.

Latching onto a through ball from Paul Shaw, the Oxford hitman's effort was smothered well by the on-rushing Nikki Bull.

Oxford would rue the missed chance as Aldershot broke quickly out of defence. Louie Soares burst past his marker and found John Grant in space on the right. With Billy Turley bearing down on him, the livewire frontman left the Oxford keeper for dead, turning neatly inside and slotting home the coolest of finishes.

The goal sparked chants of "What a load of rubbish!" from the Oxford supporters and their mood was not helped by the cries of "The Shots are going up!" from the away section.

The half-time whistle was greeted with a combination of angry boos from the home crowd and triumphant cheers from the red and blue army.

But Smith knows how to conduct a half-time team talk, and he certainly produced some words of wisdom for his Oxford players. Within 30 seconds of the restart, the home side had pulled a goal back, Alex Jeannine volleying a right-wing cross home.

Ten minutes later the scores were level when Paul Shaw produced a neat finish after latching on to a Yemi Odubade flick.

After looking so composed in the first period, the Aldershot defence was now under pressure, with the pace of substitute striker Odubade causing problems for Charles and Winfield.

After 66 minutes, things got worse when Charles limped off, Rob Gier replacing him at centre-back and Soares moving to right-back.

Oxford had a golden opportunity to take the lead after

22   The Shots are Back

Dave Winfield battles for the ball.

© Oxford Mail

"Oxford are a big club and among the favourites to go up, so we're delighted to come here and get the three points. We played well first half. We were organised, we were fluid and we worked really hard."

Gary Waddock

76 minutes when Shaw played another through ball to Robinson, but for the second time in the match Bull produced a wonderful save to deny him.

However, committing so many men forward, Oxford were always vulnerable on the break. With seven minutes left, a Davies corner from the right was headed home by Lewis Chalmers, sending the travelling supporters into delirium and cementing second place in the table for Aldershot.

ALDERSHOT TOWN 2

(Davies 57, Elvins 73)

YORK CITY 0

LINE-UP
Bull, Gier, Straker, Day, Winfield, Chalmers (Newman 70), Soares, Davies, John Grant, Elvins, Harding.

Returning skipper Rhys Day challenged his five-star Shots to make the most of their excellent start and push on for a promotion challenge.

With their fifth win in succession, the Shots have cemented their place in the play-off spots, sitting just one point behind leaders Stevenage.

Now with the whole of the Blue Square Premier starting to sit up and take notice of his side, Day claims he never had any doubt that Aldershot had what it took for a promotion push.

> **"** *From the minute the gaffer got the team together we always knew we had quality and we had a chance.* **"**
>
> Rhys Day

"Now we've stamped our authority on the league table we've got to kick on and make sure all this hard work we've put in doesn't go to waste."

Following on from the impressive away win at Oxford on Saturday, Waddock was forced to make one change, replacing the injured Anthony Charles with Day, who had sat out the Oxford match with an injury of his own.

Aldershot were still full of energy after Saturday's win. With a little too much haste in their play, they were ragged and frantic for much of the first half. Often guilty of over-complicating their play, Aldershot regularly gave the ball away in dangerous positions, and York might have taken the lead early on.

York's Chris Beardsley should have put his side ahead, but instead skied his shot into the relieved East Bank.

Then, on 34 minutes, Beardsley cut in from the right, skipping several half-hearted challenges, but his left-footed shot was straight at Nikki Bull. Next up, Beardsley blasted a low shot just wide from ten yards.

The second half started as the first had ended, with an edgy Aldershot often looking vulnerable.

Ten minutes in, the impressive Rob Gier was on hand again to rescue his team when he headed off the line. However, just as an upset was starting to look possible, the Shots got a huge slice of luck.

After Louie Soares had been brought down to the left of the penalty area, Scott Davies whipped in a fierce free kick that Nicky Wroe could only head into his own goal. The dead-ball specialist will no doubt claim it was his sixth goal of the season, although it is debatable whether the strike was even on target before the deflection intervened.

What is certain, though, is that the home side now had the confidence to settle down and play the football befitting a club challenging for promotion. The introduction of Ricky Newman helped, the midfielder using his experience to calm down some of his younger colleagues.

With their play slicker and the passing crisper a second goal always seemed likely, and after 72 minutes the match was put beyond doubt. Anthony Straker made what is now a familiar marauding run down the left flank, and after beating his marker, the full-back lifted a perfect cross to Rob Elvins who headed in powerfully at the back post.

Rob Elvins' header secured the 2-0 win for the Shots.

" They [York] are a good team. We knew before the game that they're in a false position. We gave possession away far too often tonight but that will improve with the more games we play... I think sometimes because it's a young group they are a little bit nervous at home. They want to do well in front of the home crowd and it's a bit tense. When we scored tonight we relaxed a little bit. We need to relax when it's 0-0. "

Gary Waddock

ALDERSHOT TOWN 4

(Elvins 30, John Grant 47, 84, Newman 60)

FARSLEY CELTIC 3

(Gareth Grant 52, Heath 55, Downes 79 pen)

22 September 2007

Playing in their first season in the Blue Square Premier League, the Yorkshire part-timers were applauded off the pitch by the Aldershot faithful after giving a superb account of themselves in an extraordinary seven-goal thriller that saw both sides go for the win.

With the same team that defeated York City the previous Tuesday, Aldershot started in a now familiar nervy fashion, with the visitors having several early opportunities to take the lead.

After just two minutes, the ball found its way to Gareth Grant on the left but his shot was straight at Nikki Bull. The Aldershot defence was breached twice more, first by Damian Reeves on 11 minutes with a tame shot straight at Bull, and again ten minutes later, this time by Amjad Iqbal playing in Grant. The lively striker showed electric pace to get past David Winfield, but again Bull rushed out to save his teammates.

Although controlling much of the possession, Aldershot took half an hour to create their first chance. Having found himself out on the left wing, Louie Soares lifted a cross to the back post that picked out Rob Elvins. The striker's downward header slipped past Tom Morgan in the Farlsey goal, much to the relief of the nervous home crowd.

But the Shots still looked ragged.

The dangerous Soares produced a magical run as he beat three defenders cutting in from the right. His shot did not match the build-up, however, as his left-footed drive drifted well over the bar.

In injury time in the first half, Farsley should have levelled the scores. A whipped Carl Serrant free kick from the left was met by the unmarked Colin Heath, but his header drifted agonisingly wide of the Aldershot post to let off the home defence.

If Farsley had felt hard done by at the break, their sense of injustice was compounded in the first minute of the second half.

After a neat interchange between John Grant and Scott Davies, the on-loan midfielder played in Grant, who calmly slid the ball under Morgan to double the lead.

With the Shots now apparently cruising, few people in the Rec would have envisaged the drama that was to follow.

On 52 minutes Ben Harding needlessly gave the ball away inside his own half. His loose pass was picked up by Chris Billy, who picked out Gareth Grant with a perfect through ball. After wasting an earlier opportunity, the Celtic forward took the ball around Bull to leave him with an easy finish into an empty net.

Just a minute later, Farsley beat the Aldershot offside trap, this time with Grant being sent through by Reeves. However, diving at the feet of the Celtic striker, Bull made his best save of the game.

But in the 55th minute, a Roy Stamer cross from the left was headed in by Heath. With the visitors gaining confidence it seemed the game was slipping away from the Shots, but the introduction of veteran midfielder Ricky Newman changed the match.

His calming influence and 'back to basics' approach settled his young colleagues, although on the hour mark Newman produced a rather unfamiliar piece of magic to turn the match back in Aldershot's favour.

John Grant is congratulated by Rob Elvins (left) and Lewis Chalmers.

A long Lewis Chalmers throw from the left was only half cleared by Iqbal, and the waiting Newman lashed in a fierce volley from the edge of the area.

It was the former Crystal Palace man's first goal in 52 games for the Shots, and had apparently grabbed the three points.

Farsley, however, had other ideas and on 78 minutes they were back in the game. A seemingly innocuous tussle between Grant and Davies was deemed worthy of a penalty by referee Rodeta, but Stephen Downes wasn't complaining as he calmly converted to Bull's right.

There was still time for a hero though, and with six minutes left John Grant did what he does best. After being played in by a through ball from Chalmers, Grant lifted a delightful chip over the on-rushing keeper to deny Farsley a deserved point.

> **"**Good sides are solid at the back and throughout the team, and on today's performance we weren't. We were all over the place. We came out on top, but performance-wise it was not good enough for what I want.**"**
>
> Gary Waddock

CAMBRIDGE UNITED 1
(Rendell 21)

ALDERSHOT TOWN 1
(Winfield 87)

25 September 2007

LINE-UP

Bull, Gier (Smith 54), Straker, Day, Winfield, Chalmers, Soares, Davies (Joel Grant 66), John Grant, Elvins, Harding.

© Cambridge Evening News

Rob Gier times a tackle perfectly.

An 87th-minute header from Dave Winfield against promotion rivals kept Aldershot's unbeaten away record intact, once again underlining the desire of Gary Waddock's young charges.

Naming an unchanged team for the third match running, Waddock was looking to preserve a perfect away record. But Cambridge also had the Blue Square Premier's only unbeaten record to preserve.

However, if the crowd of more than 3,500 expected two in-form sides to attack from the off, they were disappointed. Cambridge looked dangerous down the flanks but it was Anthony Straker, Rob Elvins and Scott Davies, who came closest to opening the scoring.

As it was, an ex-Aldershot player, Scott Rendell, claimed the first goal, tucking home Daniel Gleeson's cross inside the six-yard box in the 21st minute.

Elvins scored ten minutes later, but it was harshly ruled out for a foul on Cambridge keeper Danny Potter.

The Shots were actually fortunate not to go in at the break two goals down. First Nikki Bull saved well from

Rendell and then Leo Fortune-West crashed a header against the bar from Courtney Pitt's cross.

Bull made further impressive saves from Gleeson and Pitt in the second half, before the Shots came back into the game in the last half hour, now helped by Dean Smith's pace down the right flank. The Shots were adamant they should have had a penalty for a handball but their protests were waved away.

Waddock then threw on Joel Grant for his second debut for the club after last season's loan spell, and his pace and trickery caused the Cambridge defence all manner of problems, especially for Gleeson. Fittingly, with just three minutes to go and after the Shots missed a succession of half-chances, it was Grant who made space and lifted a cross into the area, which Winfield rose to crash in off the underside of the bar.

Winfield celebrated with his father behind the goal, while the jubilant Shots supporters chanted: "That's why we're top of the league!"

There was still time for Cambridge sub Marvin Robinson to be dismissed with two yellow cards in two minutes, as the Shots comfortably held on to their point.

The 100 per cent away record may be gone and, on the night, Torquay's win at Weymouth may have pushed Aldershot into second in the table, but Waddock's men clearly have the stomach for a battle.

> **"I'm pleased with the way we went about our performance, particularly in the second half. It was obvious to everyone that we deserved the equaliser."**
>
> Gary Waddock

2 October 2007

ALDERSHOT TOWN 2
(Soares 78, Joel Grant 81)

EXETER CITY 0

Aldershot once again showed that they have a taste for victory in a hard-fought win over Exeter City.

In a scrappy match that rarely produced the kind of flowing football that the Shots have so often shown this season, Gary Waddock's men were forced to dig in against a dogged and defensive Exeter side that had drawn five of their previous six matches.

But late goals from Louie Soares and super sub Joel Grant extended Aldershot's unbeaten run to eight matches and sent them flying up to second in the table.

After last Tuesday's dramatic late equaliser at Cambridge, Waddock made one change to his side, bringing in Dean Smith, just declared fit, at right-back in place of Rob Gier.

With only one up front, Exeter's desire to stifle the match was clear from the start. Goal scoring opportunities were at a premium, with play often breaking down due to sloppy passing in the Aldershot midfield.

On ten minutes, Lewis Chalmers launched a monstrous throw from the right that found David Winfield unmarked at the far post. However the big centre-back seemed to be taken by surprise and was unable to control the ball.

Playing a new midfield set-up, Waddock moved Ben Harding in to centre midfield, with Scott Davies switched to the right wing.

The tactic almost paid off on 20 minutes when Harding unleashed a powerful 20-yard drive that was deflected just wide of the Exeter goal.

Just after the half-hour mark, Exeter finally began to apply some pressure on the Aldershot goal. First, lone striker Jamie Mackie wriggled in from the right and

fired in a low drive that was straight at Nikki Bull. Three minutes later, a Dean Moxey corner from the right was headed just wide by Jon Richardson.

Despite seeing little of the ball, Aldershot nearly took the lead on 38 minutes when Rhys Day's towering header was cleared off the line by Matt Gill.

The second half began in a similar vein, with first George Friend and then Lee Elam putting good chances wide of the Aldershot goal.

The Shots had an opportunity of their own after 52 minutes when Rob Elvins was sent clear on the left flank. The in-form striker never looked convincing though, and his scuffed effort drifted wide of Andy Marriott's post.

Three minutes later most of the Recreation Ground thought the Shots had made the breakthrough.

The Shots celebrate Louie Soares' goal.

Super sub Joel Grant seals the points.

After a fierce challenge by Chalmers on the edge of the Exeter penalty area, the ball found its way to Soares on the right. The winger slid the ball calmly past Marriott but, with the Shots supporters already celebrating, his effort rebounded back off the post.

At this point, many may have started to think that it was not Aldershot's night, and a smash and grab effort by the visitors was starting to look possible. However it

was Exeter's counter-attacking that would prove to be their undoing.

On 77 minutes, Elam turned Winfield brilliantly to put himself in on goal. But as he has done so often this season, Bull rushed out of goal to make a dazzling save. Not content with that, Bull then quickly threw out to Soares on the right, who flew up the wing in familiar fashion.

Cutting in from the flank, Soares then skipped across the Exeter area and whipped a superb drive back across goal that flew into the Exeter net.

Just three minutes later, the Aldershot crowd could really relax thanks to some more magic from substitute Joel Grant. The former Watford man had changed the game at Cambridge a week before, and his trickery and skill once again proved decisive for the Shots.

Picking up the ball on the left, Grant produced a double step-over that bamboozled his marker, before unleashing a stunning strike that slammed into the top corner of the Exeter goal.

Although the goal gave the scoreline a slightly flattering look for Aldershot, it sealed another battling win for the Shots.

6 October 2007

STEVENAGE BOROUGH 3

(Winfield og 24, Arber 45 pen, Dobson 46)

ALDERSHOT TOWN 1

(Day 48 pen)

It was the same team that battled to victory the previous Tuesday against Exeter, with one exception.

With star striker John Grant missing through tendonitis in his knee, boss Waddock brought in the hitman's young Jamaican namesake, Joel Grant, who had been so impressive in his two substitute appearances since joining from Watford.

Apparently buoyed by their eight-match unbeaten run, Aldershot started brightly, with Grant taking just four minutes to tease the Stevenage full-back with his trademark step-overs. After getting to the byline, Grant pulled back to Louie Soares, who had his scuffed effort cleared off the line.

On 19 minutes, a familiar long throw from Lewis Chalmers was met by the head of David Winfield, but saved comfortably by Alan Julian in the Stevenage goal. Two minutes later, Aldershot again went close, this time a looping header by Soares that drifted inches over the bar.

Soon after, Aldershot should have taken the lead when a chip in the area by Chalmers was met by Winfield. The big centre-back headed across goal towards Rob Elvins, who somehow had his effort cleared off the line by Steve Morison.

Despite dominating play, the Shots were unable to find the breakthrough, and after 24 minutes they were made to pay for their wastefulness.

After Daryl McMahon skipped past Dean Smith on the left, his whipped low cross was met by the outstretched leg of Winfield, who could only divert the ball past Nikki Bull and into the Aldershot goal.

Borough now upped the pace.

On 27 minutes, Mitchell Cole's cross from the left was met by John Martin, who shot straight at Bull when he should have done better.

Although struggling on the right wing again, Scott Davies went close with a bending free kick on 44 minutes.

Then, after good chances at either end, Winfield clumsily pulled down Cole in the Aldershot area. The referee immediately signalled a penalty, which Mark Arber convincingly slotted home in front of the travelling red and blue army.

After numerous battling comebacks this season, Shots supporters would have been looking for a response in the second period.

However, just a minute into the second half, Cole streaked past the hapless Winfield before playing in Craig Dobson, who finished comfortably for Borough's third.

Two minutes later, Ben Harding was brought down by ex-Shots man Mark Molesley, and skipper Rhys Day made no mistake with a well-taken penalty to give Aldershot hope.

Stevenage were in no mood to sit back on their lead, and on the hour mark, Morison dispossessed Winfield on the left and crossed to Cole, who somehow saw his effort kept out with a remarkable save by Bull.

Generous defending from the visitors presented McMahon and Cole with further opportunities to put the game beyond doubt, before substitute Kirk Hudson sliced an effort wide of the Borough goal.

On 71 minutes, McMahon split the Aldershot defence with a through ball to Cole but, for the umpteenth time this season, Bull rushed out to smother the shot.

Bull's best efforts weren't enough to keep Stevenage from finding the back of the net.

© The Comet, Stevenage

A minute later, Stevenage had the opportunity to seal the win when yet more calamitous defending saw Bull bring down Cole in the area. This time, however, the Shots' stopper guessed correctly and saved Arber's effort with a full-stretch dive to his left.

Following the introduction of Hudson and Jonny Dixon, Aldershot looked lively on the counter attack, with Day heading wide and Julian in the Stevenage goal producing wonderful saves to keep out Soares and Dixon.

However, Stevenage held on for the three points that sees them leapfrog Aldershot into second place in the Blue Square Premier Division.

> "It was an open game and I'm sure the fans enjoyed it. It's probably the best we've started in a game. We had a couple of opportunities and if we had taken one of them maybe it would have been a different outcome. We played well in patches and we presented them with the goals, but we're not too downhearted and we'll be OK."
>
> Gary Waddock

ALDERSHOT TOWN 2
(Day 71 pen, Soares 86)

EBBSFLEET UNITED 0

LINE-UP

Bull, Smith, Straker, Day, Winfield, Chalmers (Davies 56), Soares, Harding, Dixon, Elvins (Hylton 65), Hudson (Newman 77).

On a night when Aldershot welcomed home the Grenadier Guards from Afghanistan, the players seemed keen to put on a show for the returning servicemen, attacking Ebbsfleet from the off.

After just three minutes, Ben Harding found space on the edge of the visitors' penalty area with a neat turn, but his curling shot flew over the bar.

Ebbsfleet, however, were in no mood to sit back and defend. Playing with two strikers (rare for recent away sides at the Recreation Ground), United carved out a number of openings themselves.

On seven minutes, Stacy Long whipped in a cross from the left which was met by Chris McPhee, but the former Aldershot loanee's header was just wide. Two minutes later, Neil Barratt beat the Shots' offside trap to slide the ball past Bull, but his shot agonisingly rebounded back off the post.

With United pressing hard, the Aldershot midfield was having to play at a high tempo, but unlike previous matches, the Shots' passing was of a standard befitting the league leaders.

After 16 minutes, a deep Anthony Straker cross from the left found Louie Soares unmarked at the back post. But despite having time to bring the ball down, the winger rushed his volley which sailed high over the bar. Again, six minutes later, Soares was sent clear by Rob Elvins only to hurry his effort, his lob drifting wide.

Aldershot kept up the pressure and on 28 minutes, a low cross from Hudson on the left found Elvins in the box who, after controlling well, fired his shot straight at Lance Cronin in the United goal.

Although attacking well, the Shots still looked nervous in defence, and after 43 minutes Nikki Bull underlined his importance to the side with a superb double save.

As the Aldershot defence failed to clear the ball, McPhee fired in a powerful shot that was well saved by Bull. Then as Luke Moore looked to pounce on the rebound, the Shots' stopper threw himself bravely at the feet of the United striker.

There was still time for Elvins to curl an effort just over the bar, before reaching a frustratingly goalless half time.

Following the half time tributes to the returning armed forces, Jonny Dixon took just two minutes to force the Ebbsfleet keeper into action when he saw his half-volley tipped over the bar.

The visitors still harboured their own ambitions of opening the scoring, and just after the hour mark they should have been ahead.

After McPhee fed Raphael Nade on the left, the striker turned Dean Smith inside out before crossing in to Mark Debolla in the Aldershot area. But with the goal at his mercy, the midfielder hesitated, lifting his shot well over the bar when he should have done better.

With the Aldershot defence getting more nervy by the minute, the feeling of anxiety seemed to transfer itself to the crowd, who were starting to consider the possibly of maiden back-to-back defeats this season.

Clearly needing a bit of luck, the Shots got it in the 69th minute.

After Harding had spread play with a fine lofted ball to Soares on the right, the winger lifted a cross in towards

Elvins at the far post. As the former West Bromwich Albion man attempted to meet the cross, Mark Ricketts inexplicably hauled down the striker, leaving referee Hopkins with no option but to award a penalty.

Skipper Rhys Day accepted spot-kick duties, and after confidently slotting home against Stevenage on Saturday, the centre-back again gave a masterclass in finishing, lifting the ball high into the Ebbsfleet net.

With one goal not enough to secure fully the points, Aldershot went looking for a second, and with eight minutes left, Harding should have sealed the win.

Yet another dangerous cross by Soares from the right was flicked on by Elvins to an unmarked Harding. But despite having all the space and time he needed, the young midfielder fired his volley high over the bar into the East Bank.

Just a minute later, Bull once again produced a world class one-on-one save to rescue his side after Nade had been sent through by John Hastings.

With four minutes remaining, Ebbsfleet were made to pay for their misses when Soares netted at the third time of asking.

Two Aldershot substitutes combined when Ricky Newman lifted the ball out to Danny Hylton on the right. After getting to the byline, the young forward pulled the ball back to Soares, who this time made no mistake to grab his third goal of the season and seal the win.

Louie Soares in the thick of it.

13 October 2007

BURTON ALBION 2
(Webster 10, Greaves 51)

ALDERSHOT TOWN 0

Louie Soares created plenty of chances, but couldn't quite deliver.

© Burton Mail

Having built up an unbeaten record of six matches on their travels, including five wins, Aldershot Town turned in their worst performance of the campaign and succumbed to their second successive away defeat of the season after a disappointing display at Burton Albion.

This was the first time that the Shots have lost a league match against Burton in nine encounters.

The Shots were without pacy right-back Dean Smith, due to the recurrence of a knee injury that kept him out earlier in the season, Scott Davies thanks to a heel injury, and John Grant, on the sidelines with tendonitis.

Burton were the quicker team out of the starting blocks. Tricky left-winger Keith Gilroy had already set up a couple of scoring chances for Burton before his tenth-minute corner was met by the head of Aaron Webster. He powered the ball into the net in convincing fashion from the edge of the six-yard box, giving goalkeeper Nikki Bull no chance.

The Burton players' confidence was boosted, although their attractive attacking play was not being converted into meaningful chances. Webster could have added a second goal on 20 minutes, but headed Gilroy's cross just over the bar.

Just three minutes later Burton should have doubled their lead.

Daryl Clare and Mark Greaves worked a neat one-two down the right before Clare played in Andy Corbett on the edge of the area. Corbett beat his man and looked set to score, but his low shot flashed just past the far post.

Shortly afterwards, Aldershot created a rare chance when Jonny Dixon received the ball on the edge of the six-yard box, but his placed shot was anticipated by goalkeeper Kevin Poole, whose smart save belied his 44 years.

There were more efforts on goal at the other end as Greaves placed a header wide, and Edwards also managed to miss the target with a snap shot.

Burton largely controlled possession for the rest of the half, although just before the break Dixon and Louie Soares worked well together down the left-hand side, only for a Soares shot to go directly into the arms of keeper Poole.

Once the second half got under way, Burton were quick to resume their attacking ways and on 51 minutes they

scored a deserved second goal, albeit from a disputed corner.

Soares let the ball run out of play, confident that it was going for a goal kick, but referee Colin Harwood, who enjoyed a good game, thought otherwise and awarded a corner.

Gilroy provided the perfect delivery for Greaves to power home a header, and with the score at 2-0 after 51 minutes, there seemed little chance of the Shots getting back into the game.

Indeed within five minutes of the goal, Gilroy unleashed a 20-yard shot that brought out the best in the visitors' keeper.

The home team appealed vociferously for a penalty in the 61st minute when Anthony Straker seemed to prevent the ball reaching an unmarked Jake Edwards with his arm, but play continued.

Burton have a knack of scoring late goals, with 13 of their season's tally having come in the final 20 minutes. But Aldershot's never-say-die attitude saw them enjoy their best spell of the game in the last quarter of the match.

Substitute Danny Hylton, who replaced Dixon as part of a triple swap on 55 minutes, was a lively addition to the team, with his energetic style never allowing his marker to settle.

It was Hylton who had two decent chances in the final ten minutes, with Poole parrying one 12-yard effort into the path of Soares who failed to convert from six yards.

Poole then pulled off another good save when Hylton shot low to the keeper's right as the Shots searched for a way back into the game which never materialised.

The defeat leaves them in second place in the league, two points behind Torquay.

20 October 2007

ALDERSHOT TOWN 1
(Dixon 90)

HALIFAX TOWN 0

Jonny Dixon's goal deep into injury time grabbed all three points for the Shots, who were poor on the day.

Still, while the football may not have been pretty, Saturday's below-par display showed once again that Gary Waddock's side can battle.

A refusal to give up until the final whistle and fitness levels to match a gritty and determined attitude were the key factors in this victory.

Luck also played its part for Aldershot in this match. Halifax had a shot cleared off the line, Nikki Bull made several testing saves look easy, the Shaymen had a man sent off, and Dixon's goal came right at the end of five minutes of added time.

> " *Football is a 95-minute game these days.* "
>
> Gary Waddock

Last season Halifax dominated for long periods at the Recreation Ground, only to lose to a last-minute winner

Jonny Dixon scrambles for the ball.

from Darren Barnard. History repeated itself in this match, leaving Halifax with another long trip back to Yorkshire, empty-handed.

The dismissal of Jake Wright in the 53rd minute, for two bookings, was possibly key as Halifax were to tire late on. But Wright's second offence – swearing after the Shots were awarded a penalty for an alleged handball by Steve Bushell – was not immediately punished, as Rhys Day screwed his spot-kick wide of the left post.

Aldershot came into the game with a lengthy injury list, missing John Grant, Anthony Charles and Scott Davies, not to mention Ryan Williams and Ryan Scott. They laboured in the first half and were indebted to yet more great goalkeeping from Bull and a superb clearance off the line by Dave Winfield, from Lewis Killeen's shot.

On the rare moments that Aldershot did press forward, they could not unsettle Halifax's strapping centre halves, Adam Quinn and Grey Young.

Still, Aldershot's strength in numbers did begin to tell in the last half an hour, especially once Waddock had thrown on an attacker – Kirk Hudson – in place of Day. Hudson's pace and willingness to run at players made him a real handful, although he needs to produce such form across 90 (or should that be 95?) minutes, rather than just as an 'impact' player from the bench.

Another substitute, Joel Grant, mustered Aldershot's

first shot on target, in the 83rd minute. And it was ten-man Halifax who came closest next, with Matt Doughty forcing a fine save from Bull.

But, with just ten seconds to go, Dixon stole the points, converting Hudson's cross in off the post. Halifax's players sank to their knees, while Aldershot's hit the floor too, converging in a happy heap on Dixon.

> "The lads have got a never-say-die attitude. There are always opportunities late in games. I don't mind when the goals come and we will gladly take the win."
>
> Gary Waddock

27 October 2007
FA Cup Qualifying
Fourth Round

CRAWLEY TOWN 1
(Carayol 30)

ALDERSHOT TOWN 1
(Dixon 55)

A dominant second-half display ensured that Aldershot live on in the FA Cup, after coming from behind in Saturday's fourth qualifying round tie to bring Crawley Town back to the Recreation Ground for a replay.

The winners of that match, which will go to extra time and penalties if required, will face more Blue Square Premier opposition in the first round, away to either Stafford Rangers or Cambridge United on the weekend of 10-11 November.

Jonny Dixon, who played on loan from Wycombe Wanderers for Crawley in 2003, scored the all-important equaliser in the 56th minute after another Crawley loan signing from the Football League, Mustafa Carayol of MK Dons, had curled Crawley ahead on the half hour, on his debut.

In good cup tradition, the home side tore into Aldershot in the opening exchanges, urged on by a boisterous home support, some animated instructions from Red Devils' boss Steve Evans and the incessant bellows of his assistant Paul Raynor.

Not that the Shots were lacking support, of course, with at least a third of the crowd of almost 2,000 in the Broadfield Stadium cheering on the men in dark blue. And those Shots fans saw plenty of action in the goalmouth in front of them in the first 20 minutes, as Aldershot keeper Nikki Bull again excelled.

With star defender Pablo Mills absent, recalled from his loan spell by Rotherham United, Evans had announced on the club website before the game that he had signed another loan player 'from a top club, who brings real quality'. Evans told the Red Devil fans,

" *You will be over the moon once you see him play.* "

Carayol's identity was only revealed when the team sheets were issued at 2pm. While a player with just three minutes' play for MK Dons, and that against Peterborough United in the Johnstone's Paint Trophy, wasn't perhaps the big name Evans had implied, the Gambia-born left-winger enjoyed an excellent first half.

Twice in the first six minutes he delivered enticing crosses that Bull had to react quickly to smother. Guy Madjo, Crawley's prolific leading scorer, swivelled and thumped a volley just wide on 17 minutes but did little else all afternoon, excellently marshalled by Ricky Newman, who was playing in central defence for the Shots, with David Winfield rested.

Indeed, Newman's calm presence was just what was needed in a hectic tie and, by moving him back, Gary Waddock was able to draft in the fit-again Scott Davies to central midfield.

Aside from a Ben Harding shot over the bar in the opening exchanges, Aldershot barely got out of their half in the opening 20 minutes. But, as right-back Rob Gier increasingly got to grips with Carayol's pace and trickery, the Shots began to play the better football.

Dixon should have scored in the 22nd minute, but his header from Louie Soares' looping cross lacked conviction and was cleared off the line by Glenn Wilson. Four minutes later, Aldershot counter-attacked quickly and Harding would have been clear on goal if Davies had not underhit a simple pass.

The Shots were made to regret their profligacy when Carayol, given too much space on the edge of the box, jinked back on to his right foot and curled a perfectly-placed shot around Rhys Day and into the bottom corner. Just when Aldershot were looking the better side, they had been caught out by a touch of class. It was only thanks to Bull that the half-time deficit wasn't more, when he got a strong hand to Pierre Joseph-Dubois' angled shot in the 38th minute.

The Shots were much improved after the break, with Day going close with a header from a corner in the 48th minute. Crawley seemed happy to sit on their lead and the Shots duly equalised when Harding, who was at the heart of Aldershot's best attacking play, slipped in Dixon and he scored his second goal in two games. He fired the ball under Crawley keeper Ashley Bayes and into the far corner, to the delight of the Aldershot hordes behind the goal.

Aldershot should perhaps have gone on to win, enjoying a number of chances in the last half hour. Waddock brought on Danny Hylton as soon as Dixon had scored and he looked livelier than Rob Elvins. Hylton came close to scoring in the 85th minute but dragged his shot wide after being put through by Harding.

Davies' volley also forced a good save from Bayes but the best chance fell to Day in the 88th minute, heading wide after Anthony Straker had won a corner.

But while the Shots were on top, it was Crawley who came closest to scoring the winner in the 70th minute. Joseph-Dubois fed Carayol in the area but this time the quality was lacking, as he blazed wide when at the very least he should have forced Bull into action. Perhaps Carayol was still feeling the effects of a magnificent crunching tackle by Gier five minutes before.

Indeed, Crawley were given a lift by Carayol's late replacement, Magno Vieira. Aldershot fans know all about him after he scored a hat-trick at the Recreation Ground for Carlisle United in the Conference three years ago, and Vieira's direct running forced Newman and Lewis Chambers into last-ditch tackles in the area in the dying minutes.

Louie Soares and Jamie Stevens keep their eye on the ball in the Fourth Round replay at the Rec.

ALDERSHOT TOWN 1
(Soares 52)

LINE-UP

Bull, Gier (Hudson 55),
Straker, Day, Newman,
Chalmers, Soares, Davies,
Dixon (Charles 90), Hylton
(John Grant 72), Harding.

CRAWLEY TOWN 0

The magic of the FA Cup was as thin on the ground as the Crawley support, but thanks to one swing of the wand that is Louie Soares' right foot, Aldershot are into the first round proper of the FA Cup.

The Shots were a long way from their best, but they just did enough to see off Crawley in this fourth qualifying round replay and set up a tough trip to Cambridge United, who beat Stafford Rangers 5-1 in their own replay that evening.

There was more good news for the Shots with the return of striker John Grant from tendonitis, on as a substitute for the last 15 minutes.

The Shots had to play the last two minutes, plus injury time, with ten men, after Lewis Chalmers was sent off for a second bookable offence. But it was the dismissal of Aldershot assistant manager Martin Kuhl, sent to the stands after a clash with his Crawley counterpart Paul Raynor on the stroke of half-time that was far more dramatic.

Raynor and his manager, Steve Evans, were enjoying plenty of banter with Kuhl and Shots boss Gary Waddock but when both Rob Gier, who had already been booked, and Crawley's James Krause slid in from distance to a 50-50 ball, Evans and Raynor were incensed and were quick to suggest that Gier be sent off.

Kuhl defended his man and, under the nose of the fourth official, appeared to make contact with Raynor and was sent to the stands. In the event, referee Scott awarded a free kick to Crawley but took no action against Gier.

Evans wanted to talk of little else other than the Kuhl incident after the match. "He [Kuhl] has punched my assistant," claimed Evans.

"It was an absolutely disgraceful act."

Waddock, sensibly, took a leaf out of the Arsene Wenger school of management by saying: "I didn't see the incident. But I'm told nothing really went on."

Back on the pitch, Guy Madjo, Crawley's leading scorer, struck two excellent shots just wide from distance, with Nikki Bull beaten.

But at least the Shots became more threatening after the half hour. First Jonny Dixon put Soares through, but while his dinked shot beat Crawley keeper Ashley Bayes, it also cleared the bar.

Danny Hylton, given a start by Waddock ahead of the rested Rob Elvins, floated over a tantalising cross which a freshly shaven-headed Ben Harding was inches away from heading home.

Harding also came close with a header back across goal from a Gier cross but it bounced just wide of the post, with Bayes beaten.

Just as on Saturday, the Shots scored early in the second half. This time it was Hylton who was the creator, showing good strength and touch to feed Soares, who thumped a shot across Bayes and into the far corner.

For much of the last half hour Aldershot were forced to defend, with Evans changing his formation to 3-4-3 and throwing three up front.

Waddock withdrew Gier, bringing on Kirk Hudson, and moving Soares back to right back, where he did an excellent job.

WEYMOUTH 0

ALDERSHOT TOWN 2

(Elvins 33, Dixon 70)

2 November 2007

LINE-UP

Bull, Gier, Day, Davies, Straker, Soares, Newman, Joel Grant, Harding, Dixon (John Grant 79), Elvins (Hudson 87).

Chilly Friday nights in November are not exactly ideal for a jaunt to the beach, but with a classy 2-0 victory over Weymouth taking them back to the top of the Blue Square Premier, the Shots clearly do like to be beside the seaside.

With the gauntlet thrown down in Dorset, Gary Waddock and his Shots were able to sit back on Saturday afternoon and watch Torquay United lose at Plainmoor for the first time in the league this season. Cambridge United's 2-1 victory leaves the Shots a point clear at the top, with nigh on two-fifths of the season gone.

After rather uninspiring performances in beating Halifax in the league and Crawley, via a replay, in the FA Cup, plus defeats at Stevenage and Burton, the Shots rediscovered their scintillating early-season away form at the Wessex Stadium.

Weymouth struggled to create all game and had just one good chance across the 90 minutes, when Conal Platt shot wide early in the second half, when the Shots led 1-0.

Aldershot could easily have had more to show than Rob Elvins and Jonny Dixon's goals, which came midway through each half. Weymouth keeper John Stewart made two excellent first-half saves and Ben Harding and Louie Soares missed presentable chances for Aldershot after the break.

Dixon's goal, in the 70th minute, completely knocked the stuffing out of Weymouth. And what a goal it was. Harding calmly controlled a loose ball in the area after a Weymouth corner and arrowed a superb left-foot pass, almost as long and straight as nearby Chesil Beach, to Dixon on the far right touchline.

Dixon cut inside, comfortably beating Joel Kitamirike (who six years ago was playing for Chelsea in the UEFA Cup) for pace and strength, before slipping the ball

under Stewart for his third goal in four games.

Weymouth manager Jason Tindall argued afterwards that Aldershot had scored both their goals while Weymouth were enjoying their best periods of the match.

He wasn't wrong, but so much the better for the Shots. Dixon's was the classic goal away from home on the counter-attack.

In the first half, Aldershot had appeared the home side, dominating possession and territory and creating a series of good openings.

Joel Grant was outstanding. Waddock had drafted him in after moving Harding into central midfield, to replace the suspended Lewis Chalmers. Harding and Davies formed an excellent axis in the middle, keeping quiet Weymouth's former Arsenal star, Paolo Vernazza, affording him none of the time on the ball he craves.

But it was Grant who was the star, giving the Terras' right-back Scott Doe a torrid evening. It was a lame Doe against a majestic stag, and Grant had his man stuck in a rut all half.

Twice, Grant skinned Doe in the first five minutes, sending in tantalising crosses. Rhys Day went close with a header from a corner and when Grant beat Doe again, Stewart made a fine save at the feet of Dixon from Grant's clever reverse pass.

From the resulting corner, Stewart made a wonderful save to his left to keep out Harding's thunderous left-foot volley.

Weymouth eventually responded and Vernazza and Gavin McCallum interchanged well with former Shot Nick Crittenden. But the Terras failed to trouble Nikki Bull and on the half hour the Shots scored the goal they deserved.

A classy 2-0 win over Weymouth puts Waddock's Shots at the top of the league.

Appropriately, it came from a foul by Doe on Grant near the corner flag. Davies knocked in the free kick, Harding's header was cleared off the line and Elvins, on the penalty spot, lashed the ball home through the crowd.

It was a sweet moment for Elvins, who has struggled to win over the Aldershot faithful since arriving from West Bromwich Albion in the summer, and was possibly only starting because Danny Hylton was injured and John Grant just fit to make the bench.

Elvins, booked late on for time-wasting, showed neat touches throughout and his late substitution by Waddock prompted warm applause from the Shots fans, which Elvins heartily reciprocated.

Tindall introduced Stuart Beavon after the break, back from injury and a virus, and for a short while Weymouth were the better side, especially when they fed James Coutts out wide on the left.

Granted, there wasn't too much to scare the Shots down on the Jurassic Coast but Beavon did force the closest Aldershot have to a dinosaur – 37-year-old Ricky Newman – into a late tackle for which Newman was booked.

Coutts was getting the better of Rob Gier and, after a superb run, he squared the ball to the unmarked Platt on the penalty spot. It was an outstanding opportunity but Bull made himself big and the target small and Platt shot just wide.

Beavon and Crittenden later forced tidy saves from Bull, but Aldershot were the more threatening team all evening and soon Harding's exquisite pass and Dixon's run and finish killed off Weymouth.

The last 20 minutes were a stroll for the Shots, with Soares and Grant swapping wings and linking neatly with Harding and Davies. John Grant came off the bench to add another 15 minutes down the road to match fitness.

At the back, this was Aldershot's third clean sheet in four and the centre-back pairing of Newman and Day was again solid. A no-nonsense, thundering late clearance from Day, which probably would have ended up as far away as Portland Bill had the stand not intervened, was indicative of the whole side's commanding performance.

CAMBRIDGE UNITED 2

(Boylan 62, Fortune-West 65)

ALDERSHOT TOWN 1

(Dixon 31)

LINE-UP
Bull, Gier, Straker, Day, Newman (Charles 44), Davies, Harding, Soares (Chalmers 69), Joel Grant, Dixon, Elvins (John Grant 62).

An injury time equaliser for Aldershot would have been harsh on Cambridge United, but that is how Saturday's entertaining cup clash at the Abbey Stadium should have finished. Instead, Joel Grant's astonishing late miss means that there will be no replay at the Recreation Ground. Gary Waddock's Shots are out of the FA Cup.

But it's not the end of the world. Extra games can burden a promotion-chasing squad, as Cambridge, currently three places behind the table-topping Shots in Blue Square Premier, may yet find out.

Just ask Ricky Newman and Scott Davies. The defender hobbled off in the first half with a back injury, while Davies was given a straight red card in injury time for petulantly throwing the ball at Cambridge winger Courtney Pitt.

Davies' moment of madness came seconds after Grant's miss and compounded the Shots' misery. Often Aldershot's best attacking outlet during the game, at just six yards out Grant had time, space and most of the goal to aim at after good work by his namesake, substitute John Grant, but somehow placed the ball wide of the right post.

Elsewhere, the Shots lacked the attacking verve they had shown at Weymouth. Ben Harding and Davies worked hard in midfield but failed to dominate, and while Cambridge spread the ball with ease, the Shots could not release their wide men.

Full-backs Rob Gier and Anthony Straker were too busy defending to bomb forward and probably the most exciting moment of the day for Louie Soares was when the tannoy announcer pronounced his name as 'Suarez'

in the pre-match reading of the teams. Sadly Soares was unable to live up to his South American billing and rather than play beautiful football he was more in the mould of Betty Suarez – aka Ugly Betty – having to concentrate on mundane defensive duties.

Lewis Chalmers, back from a one-match suspension, was left on the bench by Waddock but impressed as a substitute. In retrospect perhaps Waddock should have brought back Chalmers and not played two wingers, but it's hard to change a winning team.

Despite being on the back foot for most of the game, Aldershot carried a threat on the break throughout and took the lead through another clinical finish from Jonny Dixon on 31 minutes, his fourth goal in five games.

Cambridge, busy complaining after former Chelsea player Rob Wolleaston had been booked for diving in the box following a tussle with Newman, were caught napping by Rob Elvins' flick. Dixon was through straight down the middle and expertly threaded the ball just wide of Cambridge keeper Danny Potter, who had made a surprisingly quick return from injury, and into the far corner.

Perhaps Cambridge's defence was still adjusting to the loss of captain Mark Albrighton ten minutes before, after he had collided with teammate Mark Peters.

More significant for the Shots was the loss of Newman on the stroke of half-time. While substitute Anthony Charles did little wrong, Aldershot were less assured at the back in the second half, in Newman's absence.

But Cambridge, despite falling behind, had already dominated the tie when Newman was still fit and Jimmy Quinn's side fully deserved their win.

That the U's had 13 shots on target and Aldershot had just three is a fair reflection of the game. Quinn's side also hit the crossbar in the first half, and were it not for a string of outstanding saves from Bull, the Shots might easily have lost heavily. It was cruel on Bull that his error of judgement led to Cambridge's late winner, scored by veteran striker Leo Fortune-West in the 85th minute, soon after arriving as a substitute.

Bull came for a free kick from Stephen Reed, the former Shot loanee, but missed the ball in a mêlée of players and Fortune-West's tapped effort had just enough pace to beat the desperate lunge of Charles.

More culpable than Bull – or indeed Joel Grant for that matter – was left back Straker, who dallied on the ball in the 61st minute and allowed Cambridge back into the game to equalise 1-1.

Darryl Knights, on loan from Yeovil Town, crossed to Lee Boylan, who all afternoon had looked more lively than Cambridge's leading scorer, Scott Rendell, another ex-Aldershot loanee. He headed neatly into the corner from close range, with the rest of the Shots' defence caught out of position by Straker's error.

Considering Bull had already had to make fine saves from Wolleaston, Boylan, Michael Morrison and Reed, that Knights had hit the bar and Cambridge had had two penalty appeals turned down, the Shots could not argue that it wasn't a deserved equaliser. But Aldershot had shown some nice interplay early in the second half and the home support was just beginning to get restless when Straker made his mistake.

At 1-1 both sides enjoyed chances to win the game. Bull made a double save from Rendell while John Grant ballooned over after fine play by Chalmers and Dixon. Pitt forced another fingertip save from Bull in the 80th minute and then Chalmers almost slipped in Dixon but Cambridge keeper Potter was quick to smother the danger.

Four minutes later came, as far as the Shots were concerned, Fortune-West's unfortunate intervention. The burly striker reacted quickest after Bull had flapped and missed and the Abbey erupted.

Worse was to follow for the Shots: first Joel Grant's glaring miss and then Davies' stupidity. Seconds after Davies' dismissal came the final whistle.

ALDERSHOT TOWN 2

(John Grant 25, Harding 50)

RUSHDEN & DIAMONDS 1

(Jackson 62)

LINE-UP

Bull, Gier, Charles, Winfield (Hudson 66), Day, Chalmers, Harding, Straker, Joel Grant, John Grant, Dixon (Simmonds 90).

There may be a more famous military base elsewhere in town, but the Recreation Ground is fast becoming a new fortress for Aldershot after Saturday's eighth win in succession at home.

The three points gained from the 2-1 victory over Rushden & Diamonds keep the Shots kings of the castle in Blue Square Premier too, a point clear ahead of Torquay United.

This was a pageant of a game to boot, with the crowd of more than 3,000 royally entertained by a feast of attacking football, and scarcely a foul in sight.

The Diamonds sparkled and, after enjoying plenty of the play and creating many chances, will feel hard done by that they left with nothing after contributing so much.

The Shots created the better chances and might easily have put the game to bed after John Grant, starting his first match since tendonitis problems flared up in early October, bundled them ahead in the first half, and Ben Harding's exquisite left-foot volley increased the lead early in the second half. But after the same two players missed golden chances to increase the Shots' lead, Rushden's lively striker Simeon Jackson pulled a goal back with half an hour to play.

Both sides enjoyed chances in a thrilling finale. Grant, Lewis Chalmers and substitute Kirk Hudson all went close for the Shots, while at the other end Rob Gier, Rhys Day and the outstanding Anthony Charles all had to make vital late tackles as the Diamonds pressed, with keeper Nikki Bull also making confident late saves.

Grant's return was especially welcome and while he is still not fully fit and looked a spent force in the dying minutes, his eye for a chance was focused from the off. By the time he looped the Shots ahead in the 25th minute he had already thumped a shot against the foot of the post too.

Grant and Chalmers had come in for the suspended pair of Rob Elvins and Scott Davies, but injuries to Ricky Newman (back) and Louie Soares (hamstring) meant that Waddock had to make several adjustments. David Winfield was recalled to the centre of defence, with Charles slotting in at left-back, Straker moved to left midfield and Joel Grant to the right.

That the Shots went on to win without several key players, against an in-form Rushden side, should not be overlooked: this was a stylish and impressive victory.

Grant's goal came after Rushden had made the brighter start. Day had cleared a shot off the line from Lee Tomlin, with Bull beaten.

But Waddock's men began to get their passing game together, with the movement becoming increasingly slick and incisive. Chalmers and Joel Grant were at the heart of most of the best play. Chalmers, looking fresh despite playing in England C's win over Finland in Helsinki three days before, put in an outstanding display in the middle, with probing passing, meaty tackling and determined headers.

The opening goal owed much to Charles, who won the ball back and forced a foul near the corner flag. Harding's whipped in free kick was partially cleared, but Joel Grant's teasing cross found namesake John at the back post and he forced the ball home off head and knee.

But back came the Diamonds. Jackson, with seven goals in his last five games to his name, should have done better but blasted over. Tomlin then volleyed inches wide.

If Rushden were unlucky to be behind, five minutes into the second half they found themselves 2-0 down. Chalmers' cute pass played in Straker, who crossed into the box where Harding clipped a delicious left-footed volley high past keeper Paul Nicholls. It was a stunning strike and Harding knew it, racing half the length of the pitch in celebration. "The Shots are going up," sang the East Bank in tribute to Harding's cannonball of a shot.

But Harding was quickly brought back down to earth. Nicholls' botched clearance fell straight to him 35 yards out, but he shot wide of the open goal with his right foot. John Grant then spurned an even better chance to make it 3-0, following good work again by Straker.

The Shots were made to rue their profligacy when former Shot Jon Challinor finally woke from his slumber and fed Jackson, who finished neatly.

It was the first goal Bull had conceded in more than 400 minutes at the Rec and it brought back bad memories of last season, when Rushden came back from 2-0 down to draw 2-2 at the Rec. But not this time: the Shots are made of sterner stuff.

Waddock deserves credit for the way he rallied his troops and changed his personnel to withstand the Rushden attack, replacing Winfield with Kirk Hudson, an attacker, and moving Charles into central defence and Straker to his more accustomed role of left-back.

The Shots looked more solid. Day grew in stature but Charles was the commander, winning countless headers and crucial interceptions. And when the Shots need a crunching tackle, there's always Rob Gier to the rescue.

Tomlin was unlucky to end up on the losing side, however, denied first by Bull's save and then Charles' superb block.

At the other end, Hudson was thwarted by a fine Nicholls save after delightful interplay from Joel Grant and Harding, and Hudson also blasted over when John Grant's shot had been blocked.

An Aldershot player came closest to scoring for Diamonds but, fortunately, Bull was on hand to keep out Day's deflection towards his own goal in the last minute. At last the final whistle blew; it had never quite become a siege but the fortress had nonetheless had to withstand a concerted advance.

> "Ben Harding's been playing really well for us, contributing in all sorts of ways. His was a super goal."
>
> Gary Waddock

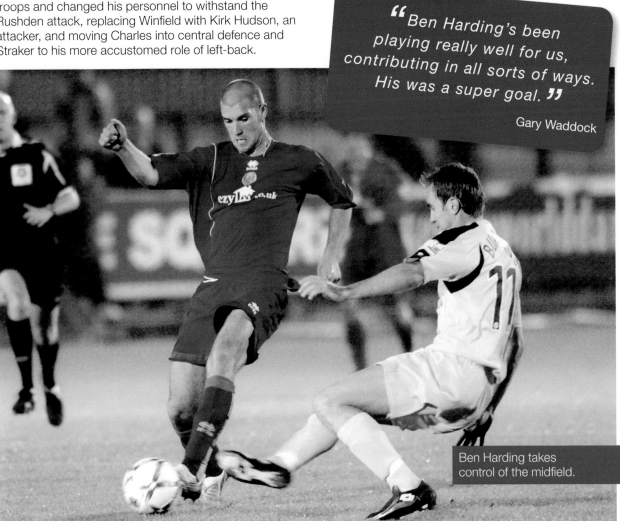

Ben Harding takes control of the midfield.

ALDERSHOT TOWN 3

(Harding 3, Dixon 40, Joel Grant 45)

22 November 2007

GRAYS ATHLETIC 2

(Gavin Grant 53, Watson 87)

LINE-UP
Bull, Gier, Straker, Day, Charles, Chalmers, Hudson (Elvins 72), Harding, John Grant, Dixon, Joel Grant.

Learning to win when not at your best is key to any successful season and Gary Waddock's table-topping youngsters look to have picked up the knack rather well.

That win briefly extended the Shots' lead at the top to four points and while Torquay United cut it back to one on Saturday, the gap between Aldershot and Burton Albion in fourth is a healthy nine points.

With most of their rivals in FA Cup action this coming weekend, and then just one more round of league matches to come before Christmas, the Shots should be sitting pretty on top of the Blue Square Christmas tree come the Boxing Day derby at Woking's Kingfield Stadium.

But this was not a convincing performance from Waddock's league leaders. It may sound strange to say that the Shots were below par, and lucky to take the three points, given that they led 3-0 at the break and scored two beautifully constructed goals in the last five minutes of the half.

But, even in that first half, Grays had enjoyed the lion's share of possession and offered plenty of potency going forward, with Aaron O'Connor a constant threat. Perhaps Aldershot shaded proceedings, just, on the back of some superb counter-attacking play, but a 3-0 advantage flattered them.

Grays dominated the second half and might easily have secured the draw that, overall, they deserved. In contrast, the increasingly nervous Shots surrendered possession time and time again, especially in midfield, and did little more than knock hopeful punts up towards the isolated John Grant.

No doubt they would have fared better with the experienced and calm head of Ricky Newman to steady the ship in the middle at the back but, to be fair to Shots captain Rhys Day, he made many a meaty header to repel Grays.

It was all hands to the pump for the Shots and it was indicative of their second half struggles that two of their best defenders were attackers, with Jonny Dixon sprinting from tackle to tackle to break up the Grays midfield and Rob Elvins, on as a substitute, making two very important late defensive headers inside his own area.

That the Shots did escape with the points owed much to two key incidents at either end of the match. Two events that were, literally, slices of luck.

First, in the third minute, Grays keeper Ross Flitney made a mockery of his side's miserly defensive away record – just four goals conceded in ten matches – by slicing a back pass behind him and leaving Ben Harding with an open goal to open the scoring.

"*It was a freak goal.*"

"Ross has been fantastic for us all season and will be again," said Grays boss Justin Edinburgh.

Perhaps, but Flitney's blunder proved decisive, gifting the Shots a goal. Then, at the death, with Anthony Straker caught like a rabbit in the headlights, unsure whether to clear the ball or play offside, Grays' Jamie Stuart was clean through on goal but rather than equalise he sliced his left foot shot wide of Nikki Bull's far post.

"That was a tremendous chance," admitted Waddock. "I'm sure Justin is very disappointed that they've taken nothing back from the game."

In fairness to the Shots, their finishing was excellent in the first half. While O'Connor twice forced Bull into fine saves, and teammates Gavin Grant and Karl Murray were a menace too, the Shots were more clinical.

John Grant had already hit the target and forced a good save from Flitney before Dixon made it 2-0 in the 40th

minute. It followed a flowing move, with Harding and Joel Grant linking well, before Dixon's shimmy opened up the space to thump a low shot past Flitney, albeit with a slight deflection off a Grays defender.

This was by far Aldershot's best period of the match. Seconds later Joel Grant curled over, and on the stroke of half time, finished off a sumptuous passage of play for a glorious goal. Kirk Hudson's incisive burst fed Lewis Chalmers, who rolled the ball to Harding. He burst towards the box and looked set to unleash a left-foot shot but, instead, faded a soft pass to Grant, who drew Flitney and slipped the ball into the corner.

Talking of corners, Grays had won as many as half a dozen in the first half and Bull and his defence had looked vulnerable from them all. So, it was of no surprise when Grays pulled a goal back early in the second half, from a corner. Bull and Day got tangled up with each other going for the ball, Straker missed a back post header, and Grant tapped into an empty net.

Although the Shots did have a few opportunities in the second half – John Grant, who still looked rusty after injury, volleyed over and failed to get a shot in when through, and Hudson had a stinging shot blocked after a clever free kick from Chalmers and Harding – Grays controlled the game.

Harding and Chalmers could not get a grip of the midfield, especially once Edinburgh introduced former Arsenal star Ian Selley. That Chalmers went on to be awarded the Man of the Match award was a surprise. He had been magnificent against Rushden a few days before but this time the composure and distribution was lacking.

It was fortunate for the Shots that Grays didn't grab a second until late in the day. O'Connor had gone close with a volley but, predictably, the goal came from another corner, which forced panic in the penalty area. Jack Obersteller smacked a shot against the post, Bull superbly saved Grant's rebound effort but substitute Luis Cumbers swept home, with the help of a deflection off Day.

The Shots fans were baying for the final whistle; Waddock was baying at his players. Still, Grays came again and Anthony Charles did just about enough to put Stuart off in a wonderful injury time chance for Grays.

The Shots had won at home, again, just. It's now eight league wins in a row at the Rec and successful promotion campaigns always require plenty of points pickpocketed from opponents.

> " We're very disappointed, but at least we won. It's far better to be a lucky manager than an unlucky one. Tonight I was a very lucky one. But so be it. "
>
> Gary Waddock

ALDERSHOT TOWN 4

(Jones 11, Elvins 31, 33, Soares 56)

CHRIST-CHURCH 0

27 November 2007
Hampshire Senior Cup

LINE-UP
Jaimez-Ruiz, Smith, Milletti, Newman, Winfield, Hardy (Koo-Boothe 76), Soares (Huggins 73), Donnelly (Sackey 69), Hylton, Elvins, Jones.

The defence of the Hampshire Senior Cup is off to a comfortable start after Aldershot enjoyed a convincing win over Sydenham's Wessex Football League outfit, Christchurch, at the Rec on Tuesday evening.

With several first team players returning from injury and suspension, boss Gary Waddock took the opportunity to give a number of players a much needed run out.

"It was important that we had this game tonight because it gave a few lads the opportunity to prove their fitness," Waddock said.

"The first team lads' attitude was fantastic and with the other boys coming in it was a good performance. They approached it in the right way and were thoroughly professional about it."

With Dean Smith back from a long injury lay-off and Ricky Newman and Louie Soares returning from two games out, plus Rob Elvins' lack of match practice following his suspension, there was plenty of first team experience on show against the part-timers from Christchurch.

The Shots took just a minute to illustrate their superiority when Soares opened up the visitors' defence with a perfect through ball to Miles Jones, but the dreadlocked winger's shot was well saved by Christchurch keeper Dan Loader.

After eight minutes, Elvins headed over from a Smith cross, but two minutes later the home side opened their account. Fed by a neat through ball from Ricky Newman, Soares got to the byline and whipped a low cross to the far post where Jones was waiting to apply a simple finish.

Just a minute later Christchurch made a rare threat to the Aldershot goal when Colin Hand picked out Lloyd Jenvey with a deep free kick, but the skipper's header flew wide of the goal when he really should have tested the Shots' number two, Mikhael Jaimez-Ruiz.

Causing all kinds of problems for the Christchurch full-backs, Soares was having fun down both flanks. After 14 minutes, a stinging 25-yard drive was well tipped over by Loader, followed by another close fire across goal, cutting in from the left. Finally, in the 31st minute, Soares received a short corner back from Scott Donnelly, lifted a cross in from the right and Elvins volleyed home.

Two minutes later, Elvins put the game beyond any doubt when he grabbed his second. After a mazy run down the left, Danny Hylton picked out Smith on the right, who crossed in for Elvins to head home to make it 3-0.

A minute before half time, Christchurch almost got on the scoresheet, but Marc Burrows' powerful drive was pushed wide by Jaimez-Ruiz.

Perhaps with last week's near-collapse against Grays still fresh in their minds, Aldershot continued to press in the second period.

In the first ten minutes of the second half, Hylton fired

into the side netting and young midfielder Donnelly twice forced good saves from Loader. In the 56th minute it was 4-0, thanks to the best move of the night.

Soares and Jones exchanged passes on the left before Soares skipped inside and placed the ball neatly past Loader from 20 yards.

With a number of players keen to impress, there was no let-up in the final quarter as Jones, Hylton and substitute Josh Huggins all had good efforts on goal.

Christchurch battled well to keep the score down, and Waddock can now look to the busy Christmas period with a fit squad to choose from, bar long-term absentees Ryan Williams and Ryan Scott.

> " It's good that we're getting the whole group together again and hopefully soon we'll be able to pick from a full squad. We're the holders of this cup and we want to win every game we play but we'll have to see how things go. "
>
> Gary Waddock

Rob Elvins gets a pat on the back from Danny Hylton for his second goal in two minutes.

SALISBURY CITY 0

ALDERSHOT TOWN 4

(John Grant 13, 81, 90, Harding 31)

LINE-UP

Bull, Gier, Straker, Day, Charles, Chalmers, Soares (Newman), Harding, John Grant, Dixon (Elvins 83), Joel Grant (Hudson 90).

After five straight wins and 16 from just 21 league games, the Shots' momentum at the top is as strong as the gale that whipped across the Raymond McEnhill Stadium all evening. Fortunately for the 507 hardy souls supporting the Shots, they had Grant's goals to warm the cockles.

The Shots' leading scorer had been taking his time to get back to full fitness after missing several weeks with tendonitis, but he was certainly firing on full cylinders again.

The first was an instinctive thrash into the roof of the net in the 13th minute, the second, a delightfully disguised chip over Salisbury keeper Ryan Clarke in the 81st minute, and the third a curling shot on the turn in injury time.

However, in reality, a 4-0 victory was a trifle flattering for the Shots, who were second best for long periods of the first half and had another excellent display by keeper Nikki Bull to thank for keeping a clean sheet.

Andy Sandell missed an excellent opportunity inside the first minute, after Joel Grant and Anthony Straker had hesitated under a swirling high ball. Sandell headed weakly at Bull when he had time and space to take the ball down and pick his post.

Two minutes later and Bull made a superb save with his feet after incisive passing from the towering Robert Matthews and Wayne Turk had opened up the Shots in the inside-right channel.

Straker, Rhys Day, Anthony Charles and Louie Soares all made vital tackles as the hosts pressed and they

The Mail, 4 December 2007.

Shots blossom on the back of Grant hat-trick

[Newspaper clipping article, partially legible]

were especially dangerous from corners, with the wind blowing the ball towards Bull's goal. But Bull was far more confident under the high ball than he had been against Grays, and in the end, it was Clarke and his defence who came unstuck from balls into the box.

As the Shots finally adjusted to the windy conditions, Soares and Rob Gier forced a throw-in near the right corner flag. Lewis Chalmers' long throw caused panic in the Salisbury area and, while Day missed his header, John Grant was waiting behind him to thump the ball home, and the Shots into a 13th minute lead.

On 31 minutes they repeated the trick, after their best period of the half. Soares' hopeful shot was blown back into play by the wind and Joel Grant forced a free kick with silky skills wide on the left. Clarke saved superbly from Jonny Dixon after Day had nodded down the free kick, but from the resulting corner, Harding passed the ball into the net helped by an acrobatic Chalmers pass.

Not that Salisbury's heads dropped at Harding's goal, with Feeney forcing Bull into an excellent save to his right in first-half injury time, and Sandell smashing a shot just over the bar.

Salisbury huffed and puffed in the second half but their only shot on target came in injury time, when Bull was again too good for Sandell. The aggrieved hosts, convinced that Sandell had been sandwiched by Dixon and Starker as he challenged Bull for a loose ball in the area in the 51st minute, had their appeals waved away by referee Sarginson, and the Shots rarely looked threatened after that.

The Shots could easily have scored more than they did in the second half. John Grant missed a tap-in from Chalmers' cross-shot, Harding forced a fine save before Dixon dragged the rebound wide, and substitute Rob Elvins also stung the hands of Clarke late on.

But when John Grant did score, it was in style. First Chalmers' excellent pass put him through and, as Clarke committed to the block, Grant chipped gloriously home in the 81st minute. Deep into injury time Chalmers fed Grant with a fortunate block and the striker caressed the ball home first time, for his hat trick and 13th league goal of the season.

By then, the wind was so strong that when Salisbury passed forward, the ball was blown back towards them. Aldershot had the wind in their sails and, looking at the table, they still do.

> " This is a good win and we seem to be finishing off teams well and have a habit of scoring late on in games, which is great. But I don't think we were at our best tonight but, yet again, we attacked with pace and energy. "
>
> Gary Waddock

HAMBLE ASSC 0

ALDERSHOT TOWN 3

(Hudson 19, 72, Donnelly 64)

4 December 2007
Hampshire Senior Cup

LINE-UP

Jaimez-Ruiz, Smith, Milletti, Newman (Huggins 86), Winfield, Hardy (Sackey 80), Davies, Donnelly, Hylton, Elvins (Read 83), Hudson.

Aldershot Town are safely through into the last eight of the Hampshire Senior Cup, after winning 3-0 away at Hamble Association on Tuesday evening.

Scott Donnelly and Kirk Hudson got the Shots off to a tremendous start, scoring two goals within half an hour of kick-off. A third goal on 64 minutes from Donnelly sealed the visitors' victory.

The Shots included a number of the first-team squad in their starting XI, including Dean Smith, Ricky Newman, Scott Davies and Rob Elvins.

"Martin Kuhl took charge for the evening," said Shots boss Gary Waddock. "He tells me that all the players' attitude was first-class throughout the match.

"It was of benefit for a number of first team players who are pushing hard for starting places in other competitions."

"We have bigger priorities this season but it's another victory."
Gary Waddock

"When we were assembling the squad we knew that we were putting together a young group who had bags of talent and pace... We are very good on the counter-attack and have clinical players to finish off moves, as we showed at Salisbury. We have a high rate of scoring from chances created and that is often the difference between winning and losing. But now we are expected to win every home game and the players must learn to deal with that. Stafford may be struggling but it will be a tough game."
Gary Waddock

8 December 2007

ALDERSHOT TOWN 4

Soares 10, John Grant 21,
Dixon 44, Davies 78

STAFFORD RANGERS 3

McNiven 8, Flynn 35, Grayson 67

Stafford's Sebastian Arnolin tackles Lewis Chalmers from behind.

Despite the pressures of Christmas present-buying, and some filthy weather to contend with, a healthy crowd at the Recreation Ground was rewarded with a deluge of goals, as Aldershot pinched the points from plucky Stafford. Winning by the odd goal in seven, the Shots are now seven points clear at the top of the Blue Square Premier, and guaranteed to be top of the table come Christmas Day. As far as the Rec faithful are concerned, that's a Christmas present money can't buy.

Not that Aldershot's defending was befitting of a team sitting pretty at the top. It verged on the comical at times (well, it is pantomime season, after all)!

Granted, captain and defensive rock Rhys Day was missing, but the Shots were stretched all game by Stafford's front two of 43-year-old player/caretaker manager Neil Grayson and David McNiven. It was hard to believe that Stafford had won just once in 24 games this season and even harder to understand that they had managed just 16 league goals, given that they beat Nikki Bull with three superb strikes.

Open and attacking games like this seldom make pleasant viewing for managers, and Waddock was very relieved to hear the final whistle. "A game like that will keep the crowd coming back but I only enjoyed it when the referee blew for full time," said Waddock.

Still, he must have been pleased with himself for introducing Scott Davies from the bench in the 71st minute, soon after Grayson's goal. Davies took just seven minutes to make his mark, thrashing a rasping right-footed free kick past Danny Alcock.

> **"***It is nice when substitutes work like that.***"**
>
> Gary Waddock

It had been a brave move by Waddock, taking off two of his more attacking players – Joel Grant and Louie Soares – to bring on Davies and Kirk Hudson.

Grayson employed a bold formation, treating attack as the best form of defence. But this was no day to be a defender. The wind was strong and the pitch slippery. For a brief period in the second half it was even treading water.

The first half was frenetic for the two keepers – an Alcock and Bull story! First McNiven beat Bull with a curling beauty from the edge of the area, but the Shots equalled this individual effort with a sublime team goal. Lewis Chalmers fed John Grant, who pulled the ball back for Soares to sweep it high into the net. The same Grant then finished off a one-two with Jonny Dixon to put the Shots ahead.

But with Aldershot giving the ball away with silly passing on the sticky surface, Chris Flynn was given the freedom of the Rec to beat Bull. The Shots are top because they score plenty of goals, however – 15 in the last five Conference games – and at the right time, too. And so it proved again, with Dixon's header, from Ricky Newman's knockdown, sending them in 3-2 at the break.

Waddock's men were nervy in the second half, but at least Grayson's dipping volley from 30 yards to equalise came with enough time left for the Shots to fashion a winner, and Davies obliged, after a foul by Richard Sutton on John Grant.

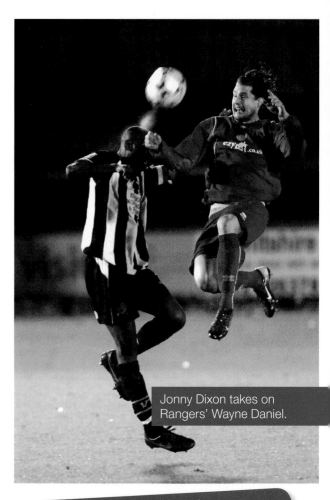

Jonny Dixon takes on Rangers' Wayne Daniel.

> **"***Our defending was poor today and we know we can do better than that. But fortunately we have plenty of players who can score goals in the team. Our target was three points and that's what we have. We keep winning and, while games like that are not good for the heart, I'll happily win 8-7 if it means we keep on getting three points.***"**
>
> Gary Waddock

Scott Davies smashes home the winner.

HAYES & YEADING UNITED 0

ALDERSHOT TOWN 5

(Davies 20, John Grant 42, Dixon 60, 72, Hudson 89)

LINE-UP

Jaimez-Ruiz, Gier (Smith 76), Straker (Charles 34), Day, Koo-Boothe, Chalmers, Soares, Davies, John Grant, Dixon, Harding (Hudson 46).

It was Arctic off the pitch but Aldershot remain red-hot on it after cruising past Hayes & Yeading 5-0 in the first round of the FA Trophy.

Shots manager Gary Waddock had said that his side would not get caught cold in this competition. And his side were true to their word, as they romped to a seventh successive victory.

Granted, 5-0 was harsh on Hayes, who started the better of the two teams, with debutant Nathan Koo-Boothe looking uncomfortable at the back and Mikhael Jaimez-Ruiz, in for the injured Nikki Bull, nervous in goal.

But once Hayes keeper Delroy Preddie had presented the impressive Scott Davies, who started ahead of Joel Grant, with the opener in the 20th minute, it was all pretty much routine for the Shots.

Jaimez-Ruiz settled down and did very well later in the game. With rumours growing that Bull may be off to pastures new in the Football League, Jaimez-Ruiz's performance will have impressed Waddock. Not that the manager believes Bull will leave. "Nikki has a slight Achilles injury," said Waddock.

" Yes, the transfer window is coming up but he is under contract to us and I've had no call about him. "

Hayes, fresh from a league win over Conference South leaders Lewes, tore into the Shots early on, hitting the post and nearly forcing Rhys Day into an own goal. But when Preddie's woeful kick went straight to Davies, the young Irishman made a difficult task look easy, passing a left-footed shot back into the empty net. It was fitting reward for Davies, starting for the first time since being sent off in the FA Cup at Cambridge. He was comfortably the Shots' best player in the first half.

Jaimez-Ruiz made good saves from former Shot Steve Perkins and both Kieran Knight and Will Hendry, before John Grant sent the Shots in 2-0 up at the break, lashing the ball home from Louie Soares' pass.

Waddock's men stepped up a couple of gears in the second half, with substitute Kirk Hudson's pace too much for the hosts. Jonny Dixon, set up by strike-partner Grant, helped himself to two goals, taking his tally to eight in the last ten games, and Hudson hooked in a fifth.

" We really stepped it up in the second half. "

"I thought there was some high quality play and finishing. It was a professional performance. Hopefully we can get a home draw in the next round," said Waddock.

" They put us under pressure early on, but the first goal was always going to be important and getting it settled us down. Jonny and John are in great form up front and long may it continue. "

Gary Waddock

ALDERSHOT TOWN 1
(Hudson 67)

OXFORD UNITED 0

22 December 2007
Setanta Shield

On a day when most people were doing their late Christmas shopping, Aldershot left it late to secure yet another victory at the Recreation Ground.

Still, a not unreasonable crowd of close to 1,600 watched the win, which came courtesy of Kirk Hudson's second-half goal.

After all, if there is a Mickey Mouse non-league cup, then the Setanta Shield is it. Gary Waddock's team selection reflected that, especially with three Blue Square Premier games to negotiate in the then days after this game. Nikki Bull, Lewis Chalmers and Ben Harding sat wrapped up in the stands, ahead of bigger challenges to come. The powerful quartet of Rhys Day, Louie Soares, John Grant and Jonny Dixon all started on the bench.

Oxford fielded something closer to their 1st XI but they are in a winter of discontent, and it showed. They have now gone six games without scoring and even lost in the FA Trophy at Tonbridge Angels last week. Their malaise is in stark contrast to the Shots, who have won 12 games in a row at the Recreation Ground and eight in a row, home and away.

> **"The whole squad is developing a winning mentality."**

"I made a few changes but the lads were committed and strove for the win," said Waddock.

This was not a game to remember, and chances were few and far between. The winner came in the 67th minute, soon after Waddock had shown his intention to avoid extra time and penalties by bringing on Soares and John Grant for the ineffective Rob Elvins and Joel Grant. As it was, it was two of Waddock's young guns, Danny Hylton and Hudson, who combined, for Hudson to finish coolly.

Oxford pressed late on but Mikhael Jaimez-Ruiz was rarely troubled, largely thanks to an inspirational display at centre-back from Anthony Charles.

> **"We just take one game as it comes."**

"Now we have the Setanta match done and dusted we can concentrate on the first of our league derbies against Woking," said Waddock afterwards.

> **"Kirk Hudson is a threat whenever he plays. He has pace and quality and took his goal really well. All he needs is a little bit more belief in himself. Martin Kuhl and I already have that belief in him."**
>
> Gary Waddock

WOKING 0

ALDERSHOT TOWN 1

(Hudson 78)

LINE-UP

Bull, Gier, Straker, Day, Charles, Chalmers, Davies (Hudson 62), Harding, Joel Grant, Dixon (Hylton 73), Elvins.

The euphoria of a narrow 1-0 victory in the opening derby game was immediately halted by the tragic news of the death of Paul Muddell, an Aldershot director.

Muddell, chairman of the Aldershot Town Supporters' Club and one of the most helpful and hardworking volunteers the club had ever seen, collapsed in the Woking boardroom straight after the match, having watched his beloved Shots cement their place at the top of the Blue Square Premier, thanks to substitute Kirk Hudson's late winner.

Despite the best efforts of the Woking doctor, directors from both clubs and the emergency services, Muddell could not be revived. The second derby, at the Recreation Ground on New Year's Day, saw a pre-match minute's silence in his memory impeccably observed.

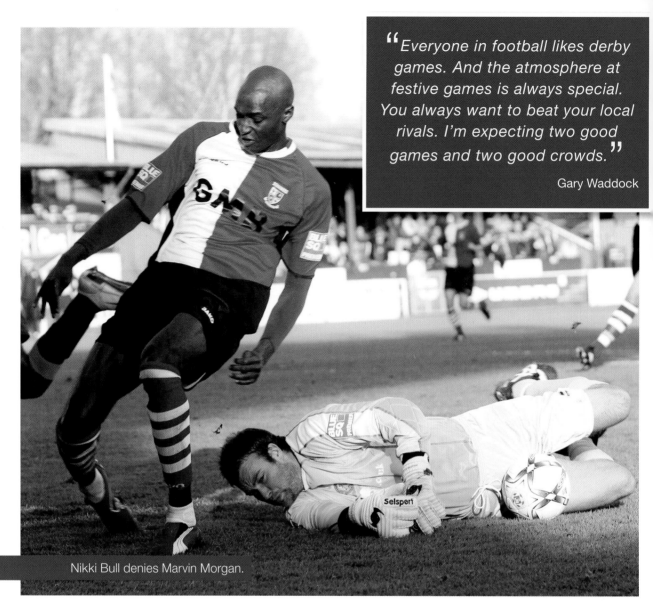

Nikki Bull denies Marvin Morgan.

Before the day's desperately sad turn with the news of Aldershot director Paul Muddell's death, it had been a very happy one for the Shots and their magnificent support. An attendance of 4,356, around 2,000 of whom were Shots fans, will have certainly put a smile on the face of Woking's financial director, despite the result.

Aldershot had needed their key men to play well, given that leading scorer John Grant and influential winger Louie Soares were both ruled out with minor knocks. But Woking had enjoyed the better of the opening stages and Shots keeper Nikki Bull, fit after an achilles problem, had to dive bravely at the feet of gangling striker Marvin Morgan as early as the fourth minute. Morgan also headed weakly at Bull in the ninth minute and hit the bar with a deflected shot ten minutes later. Three minutes after that Morgan turned Rhys Day and

Rob Gier made a superb defensive header in front of Bull.

That was probably Day's only error in what was otherwise a magnificent defensive performance. A stunning block from Giuseppe Sole's second-half shot was probably Day's finest moment, but all game he blunted Woking's best efforts with skill and controlled bravery, complementing stunning performances from Anthony Charles, Ben Harding and Lewis Chalmers.

Although Davies forced Woking keeper Nick Gindre into a fine save in the 15th minute, Aldershot's best first-half chance fell to left-back Anthony Straker. He and Jonny Dixon shared a one-two but Straker, clean through, delayed his shot and Gindre smothered the effort.

In the second half, Rob Elvins and Dixon worked hard

Joel Grant mesmerises Paul Lorraine.

and the Woking defence was beginning to tire when Waddock surprised a few by hauling off Davies and Dixon and bringing on Danny Hylton and Kirk Hudson. Hylton was particularly impressive and Waddock was delighted that his squad increasingly has such strength in depth.

Joel Grant terrorised Woking's stand-in right-back, Paul Lorraine, spurred on by the Shots fans, who hugged the whole length of the far touchline. If his finishing had been as impressive as his approach play then the Shots would have won more comfortably, as three times he shot wide when well-placed in the area.

Instead, the victory came from a double-H-ed sword from the bench. Hylton raced into the inside-left channel in the 78th minute, pulled the ball back, and Hudson, his fellow substitute, swept the ball home for his second winner in four days, after the 1-0 win over Oxford United in the Setanta Shield.

"*I don't think either side would have complained if it had finished 0-0... but were just a bit sloppy for one moment.***"**

Frank Gray, Woking manager

It was a deserved victory on the back of Aldershot's second-half dominance, although Woking showed that they will be dangerous and dogged opponents on New Year's Day.

The Shots celebrate Kirk Hudson's winner.

GRAYS ATHLETIC 2

(Obersteller 43, Watson 52)

ALDERSHOT TOWN 1

(Dixon 65)

29 December 2007

A disastrous two-minute period just before the half-hour proved decisive as Aldershot Town lost for the first time in Blue Square Premier since October 13 and for the first time in any competition since early November, going down 2-1 away at Grays Athletic.

First skipper Rhys Day had a penalty saved by Grays keeper Ross Flitney in the 26th minute and then, just two minutes later, midfielder Scott Davies was given a straight red card for a dangerous tackle.

> **" I'm not sure Scott made any contact at all. "**
>
> Gary Waddock

"It looked a bit harsh to me… I'll have to have a look at the match video," said the Shots boss.

A few months ago Davies might have escaped with just a yellow card but with dangerous, lunging tackles making high-profile news in the Premiership, it was pretty inevitable that the referee would brandish the red card for Davies' unnecessary studs up slide from behind, in the midfield. He will now serve a four-match ban after being sent off at Cambridge United in the FA Cup.

With Lewis Chalmers also facing a one-match ban next week away to Northwich Victoria, Waddock's midfield will be severely depleted should Ben Harding get injured or suspended. But Davies' absence was most keenly felt on Saturday.

The ten men of Aldershot battled bravely for the remaining hour and more, maintaining an attacking formation. Substitute Danny Hylton should have done better with a headed chance in injury time, but guided his effort too close to the safe hands of Flitney, who had enjoyed a miserable evening in Aldershot's 3-2 win over Grays at the Recreation Ground five weeks before. It needed another inspirational display from keeper Nikki Bull and some rotten finishing from Grays to keep the Shots in touch in the second half.

The Shots had looked largely in control of the match before the dismissal, with Joel Grant twice going close. Indeed, Aldershot were very unlucky not to be awarded a penalty – and perhaps see Grays reduced to ten men – in the 13th minute, when Rob Gier's goal bound shot appeared to be turned behind by the arm of Grays' Karl Murray.

When Aldershot did get a penalty, it was pretty soft. Grant cut in from the left after a fine pass by Anthony Straker and collapsed to the floor after running into Andy Sambrook. Referee Cooper's decision was harsh on Sambrook, who had simply stood his ground. With John Grant still missing with tendonitis, Day, who had missed a penalty against Halifax Town in October, stepped up but his weak kick was pushed aside by Flitney's left hand.

Despite a good chance on the break for Rob Elvins, Grays dominated the last 15 minutes of the half after Davies' sending off. Bull saved superbly from Aaron O'Connor and Jack Obersteller blasted wide. Finally, two minutes before the break, Obersteller turned in Watson's cross to put Grays ahead, after Watson had tricked his way past Gier.

With Louie Soares as well as John Grant still injured, the sending off forced a change of formation. Dixon and Elvins remained up front while just Gier, Day and Anthony Charles were left at the back, with Straker pushed forward to left midfield. "It was totally my decision to go 3-4-2," said Waddock.

wide, put off by Bull. The keeper made an outstanding save from O'Connor and then two more from Obersteller and substitute Alan Power. When Bull was finally beaten by Obersteller, Charles cleared off the line. Power and then O'Connor shot inches wide, before Bull pulled off a superb save to deny Kedwell.

Not that the Shots didn't have their chances, with Hudson shooting just over after a fine run and having a penalty appeal turned down as he was out-muscled in the box. Grays grew increasingly nervous after each moment of profligacy and Hylton nearly made them pay, with that last-gasp header. Instead the Shots lost, for the first time in the league since Burton in October, but it wasn't for want of trying.

To make matters worse for Aldershot, Torquay won 1-0 at Woking – ex-Shots striker Tim Sills scoring the goal – and the Gulls are now just four points behind Waddock's team at the top of the table.

Dixon's determination wasn't quite enough to see off Grays Athletic.

"Obviously their goal just before the break changed the half-time chat a little and the second half was always going to be open, given that we had just three at the back and were going for the win."

The Shots started the half well, with Harding and Dixon going close, but Watson struck a killer blow in the 53rd minute, getting a deflection to Danny Kedwell's shot, which wrong-footed Bull.

But Aldershot did not shrink back. Waddock introduced Hylton, Kirk Hudson and Dave Winfield for Elvins, Straker and Gier. Hudson was again impressive, pushing back Grays with his pace and direct running. Aldershot's best moments came from him and Joel Grant, who twice cut through the Grays defence. The first time, no-one read his cross into the six-yard box but the second time he fed Dixon who finished emphatically past Flitney, with still 25 minutes to go.

But most of the action was at the other end, as the Shots threw caution to the wind. Sandbrook shot inches

"It just wasn't our day at all. The players showed great character and belief and it was a great effort. It's impossible to win every game and we must make sure that we get back on a winning run...

Woking will be a very difficult derby game on Tuesday. I'm not sure John Grant and Louie Soares will be right for that one either. They haven't trained and at this time of year, with games coming thick and fast, I need players to be fully fit. We shall see how they go."

Gary Waddock

ALDERSHOT TOWN 2
(Hudson 20, Newman 27)

WOKING 1
(Sole 48 pen)

1 January 2008

> **"** *Above all today was about Paul Muddell. I told the players before the game that it would be lovely to go out and win for him. The minute's silence was fantastically observed by all and I'm sure that Paul was looking down and was very proud of the team after they got the win.* **"**
>
> Gary Waddock

Joy followed sadness at the Recreation Ground on New Year's Day, as Aldershot paid their respects to director Paul Muddell and then won in his memory, completing a festive double over Woking. The victory kept the Shots four points clear at the top of Blue Square Premier.

Gary Waddock's Shots also bounced back quickly from Saturday's 2-1 defeat at Grays Athletic, triumphing by the same scoreline. But while the Shots played some sublime football in the first half, scoring through Kirk Hudson and Ricky Newman, they were left hanging on for much of the second half, after Giuseppe Sole's penalty just after the break provided Woking with the fillip to launch concerted second-half pressure.

It was a similar game to Grays at the Rec in late November, when the Shots led 3-0 at the break but by the end were fortunate to hang on to a 3-2 victory. The win was all the more important as Torquay had already won 1-0 at home to Exeter in a midday kick-off, closing the gap at the top, temporarily, to one point.

Gary Waddock had welcomed back John Grant from tendonitis, with the leading scorer coming in for Rob Elvins. With Scott Davies starting a four-match ban, Hudson was rewarded with a start after scoring the winner on Boxing Day but Waddock sprung a surprise by resting Lewis Chalmers, who had a slight knock, on the bench and giving a start to Newman.

Waddock's changes worked a treat, with Hudson and Newman both on target but, in truth, Woking enjoyed the better of the first ten minutes, with Sole especially lively and Kevin James, who enjoyed an excellent game, prompting from midfield.

Once the Shots worked Joel Grant into play, however, they were completely dominant. Woking could not cope with the Shots' passing, pace and movement. And right-back Paul Lorraine, just as on Boxing Day, had no answer to Grant's quick feet and feints.

But it was John Grant who had a key role in the first goal, beating Woking skipper Tom Hutchinson and flicking a header to strike-partner Jonny Dixon. His slipped pass found Hudson's superb run and the 21-year-old easily beat Woking keeper Nick Gindre.

That goal came in the 20th minute, and seven minutes later it was 2-0, when Anthony Straker burst down the left wing and his perfect centre was guided beautifully into the far corner by Newman's head.

This was a purple patch for the Shots, producing waves of incisive attacks, with Ben Harding and Joel Grant linking especially well. Both Grants and Dixon came close to scoring and for a while Woking's usually watertight defence looked like it might be swamped.

But there were warning signs of what was to come. First skipper Rhys Day hobbled off with an achilles problem in the 41st minute, replaced by Dave Winfield, and then Woking striker Marvin Morgan shot into the side-netting a minute later.

Three minutes into the second half Winfield tugged back Hutchinson at a corner and the Shots had no complaints when a penalty was awarded. Sole confidently made it 2-1.

Nikki Bull had to make a fine save from James' long-range shot and even better ones from Sole's free kick and Adam Green's volley. The Shots struggled to find their fluency of the first half and gave the ball away with regularity and, crucially, Joel Grant could not force his way into the game.

But Frank Gray's decision to take off Sole for the last ten minutes was a strange one. The Shots coped fairly comfortably as Woking pushed three big men up front – Morgan, Hutchinson and substitute Liam Marum. Rob Gier did have to make one superb tackle but, for all their possession, Woking failed to create clear-cut openings.

If anything, the Shots enjoyed the better second-half chances on the break. Gindre saved well from Hudson and Straker, bursting onto John Grant's flick, hit an angled shot inches wide. Newman curled a free kick just wide on 75 minutes and, in injury time, substitute Chalmers, who came on for the hobbling Harding, shot just wide from 40 yards after a poor kick by Gindre.

> " It was a good game in front of a big crowd and we are very pleased to have got another three points. I wanted nine points from the holiday period but we had a bad day at the office at Grays. I must give the players a lot of credit for the way they bounced back. "
>
> Gary Waddock

Ricky Newman (right) is congratulated by Ben Harding and John Grant.

NORTHWICH VICTORIA 1
(Byrom 75)

ALDERSHOT TOWN 2
(Hudson 36, Joel Grant 49)

LINE-UP

Bull, Gier (Smith 90), Straker, Newman, Charles, Chalmers, Hudson, Harding, John Grant, Dixon (Hylton 90), Joel Grant (Winfield 79).

Despite peppering shots at goal throughout the game in the old salt-mining town of Northwich on Saturday, Aldershot Town eventually had to dig deep to hang on to three points.

Joel Byrom's fine left-footed volley with 15 minutes to go brought Northwich Victoria back into the game but the Shots held on for a 2-1 win, their ninth in ten Blue Square Premier matches. That extended their lead over Torquay United at the top of the table – temporarily, at least – to seven points.

Kirk Hudson – with an exquisite finish – and Joel Grant, in rather less beautiful fashion, scored the goals, either side of half time, but by the time Byrom set up a rousing finish the Shots should have been many goals to the good, with John Grant and Lewis Chalmers especially wasteful.

Indeed, with the score at 2-1, impressive substitute Aaron Burns, one of five new signings who featured for Dino Maamria's side after a spending spree in the January sales, would have been through on goal but for an unlucky ricochet. Then, in the dying moments, another substitute, Cayne Hanley, wasted two glorious chances to equalise inside five seconds.

Still, Shots boss Gary Waddock felt it had been a deserved and fairly comfortable three points against relegation-threatened opponents.

"It's another big result for us," said Waddock. "I thought we were in control in the first half and played some good stuff."

> " *While they changed their shape and came at us after the break we had more than enough chances to kill the game off.* "

The Mail, 8 January 2008.

"The main thing is that we have got the three points. It's another fantastic result away from home for us."

The Shots were without skipper Rhys Day, out with an achilles problem, so Ricky Newman moved back into central defence – picking up the captain's armband en route – allowing Chalmers to come into central midfield. Aldershot, who had thrashed Northwich 5-0 at the Rec in September, dominated most of what was a fairly insipid first half hour. They weaved some pretty patterns, with Ben Harding's poise and vision in the middle particularly impressive, but too often the play was too contrived around the box and the home side's rugged defence stood strong.

At the other end there was very little to trouble Nikki Bull, although he did look beaten by an instinctive defensive header from Newman, which flew just wide for a corner. With Louie Soares injured and Scott Davies suspended,

Hudson had been given another start on the right of midfield, although such is the striker-turned-wideman's form that he probably would have started even if the other two had been available.

He had already enjoyed a storming run into the box on the half hour when, six minutes later, a superb pass from Chalmers sent Hudson through on goal.

On New Year's Day against Woking he shot under the keeper to score; this time, on the move, he delicately and unexpectedly scooped the ball high over Victoria's keeper Scott Tynan and watched it drop perfectly into the top corner.

It was Hudson's fourth goal in five games against Blue Square Premier opposition.

Maamria moved swiftly after the break to change the pattern of the game, turning to a 3-5-2 formation and introducing Burns and Keith Barker, a man-mountain of a striker, up front. But within three minutes, Northwich were the team with a mountain to climb, after Joel Grant bundled home Jonny Dixon's cross shot in a crowded goalmouth, with the help of a deflection, after initial good work from the left by Anthony Straker.

But the two-goal platform was a base from which Aldershot could not extend their lead, despite a host of chances. John Grant should have done better from a cross from his namesake. Chalmers curled over when it looked easier to score after good work from Dixon, and was again wasteful when he headed wide Straker's superb cross. John Grant also made space for himself in the area but shot high, wide and ugly.

But the second half was far from one-way traffic, with Burns and Byrom forcing steady saves from Bull and Anthony Charles keeping the hosts at bay with a series of sterling headers and tackles. Northwich had not looked like scoring in the first half, but it happened in some style, as Byrom thumped a 20-yard volley back through the crowd and past a helpless Bull.

It could have been less frantic if John Grant's superb turn and left-foot shot had not come back off the crossbar in the 86th minute and substitute Danny Hylton had not missed a good chance in injury time, after doing all the hard work.

But, with Newman sitting calmly in front of the back four, which had been bolstered by the introduction of Dave Winfield, the Shots were pretty comfortable towards the end, until Hanley's glaring injury time misses from close range. Had he scored, that really would have rubbed salt into the wounds left by the Shots' profligacy.

> **"** Perhaps we nicked the points a little – but we've got nine points from 12 in a hectic schedule around Christmas and New Year, which is great. We march on. It's another away win too, which is important after losing at Grays last week. **"**
>
> Jonny Dixon

WOKING 2

(Norville 15, Morgan 53)

ALDERSHOT TOWN 4

(Soares 11, Charles 71, John Grant 75 pen, 85)

12 January 2008
FA Trophy

" Woking will be very keen to beat us after our two recent wins. They played very well in the second half at the Rec. It will be a tight game, I'm sure. "

Gary Waddock

If you thought that Aldershot would sacrifice the FA Trophy to concentrate on the race for promotion to the Football League, think again. Although they left it late, the Shots inflicted a third defeat on neighbours, Woking, in 17 days, in the most absorbing and exciting of the derby trilogy.

Braintree Town or Workington are up next in the last 16, at the Rec on February 2, so the Shots will be favourites to reach the quarter-finals.

Nonetheless, Woking dominated this match until the final quarter and Frank Gray and his side must still be wondering how they contrived to lose 4-2. Gray contributed to his side's downfall, taking off debutant Jason Norville on 66 minutes, with his side 2-1 up.

Presumably Gray felt that Norville, who hadn't played

since early November for Barnet in League Two, was tiring, and that the Cards' steady defence – only once this season have they let in more than one goal at home – would stand firm.

But Norville still looked fresh. As well as scoring in the first half, his partnership with Marvin Morgan had unsettled Aldershot's Rhys Day, back from an achilles injury, and Anthony Charles all afternoon, forcing them into uncharacteristic mistakes and misjudgements.

Norville's replacement Liam Marum was a lame duck – more Orville than Norville – and the Shots' defence, relieved of the Norville burden, was afforded more time and pushed higher up the pitch.

Suddenly Woking were the team on the back foot and Ben Harding and Joel Grant, Aldershot's two most creative players, began to dictate play. John Grant and Jonny Dixon, previously isolated up front, came into play. Within nine minutes the game had been turned on its head, with Charles equalising and Grant adding a penalty. The same Grant added a fourth five minutes from time to emphasise the Shots' late dominance.

But to attribute the game's dramatic change solely to the substitution of Norville would be unfair on Aldershot. The Shots' will to win and superior fitness were also key factors.

In fact, the Shots struck the first blow 11 minutes in when Soares, returning from three weeks out with an ankle injury, had reacted quickest to a ricochet on the edge of the Woking area and swept a left-foot shot into the far corner.

Four minutes later, Norville grabbed a fistful of Day's shirt before smacking a left-foot shot across Nikki Bull in the 15th minute and into the corner to equalise.

Waddock was without two outstanding performers from the previous Saturday's league win at Northwich Victoria – Kirk Hudson had a dead leg and Ricky Newman was ill – but Soares and Day were like-for-like replacements.

Woking, despite missing leading scorer Giuseppe Sole through suspension and seeing midfield dynamo Kevin James depart in midweek, deserve credit for unsettling the Shots from the off. The Cards were quick into the tackle, charged down every clearance and, with Norville showing a good touch, incisive going forward.

The gangling Morgan had been more mouse than mountain in the two league derbies but on this occasion he was strong and tricky. Matt Pattison, the former Farnborough player, was outstanding in the first half, even if he did shoot in the ninth minute when a pass to Adam Green would have put the former Fulham player clear on goal. Green's deadball delivery was also impressive and caused Aldershot problems all game.

But the Shots were not helped by some curious – to put it kindly – decisions from referee Yeo. Bull was penalised for picking up a touch from Charles that was not a back pass, but Bull, flanked by colleagues on the goal line, blocked Green's shot. After Lewis Chalmers was booked for a crunching tackle on Green that was well-timed and neither two-footed nor over the top, some Aldershot players – particularly Charles and Chalmers – lost their composure and, for a short while, concentrated more on the referee's deficiencies than their team's. Woking should have made them pay but Morgan sliced wide.

Woking dominated the opening exchanges of the second half and went ahead on 52 minutes. Captain Tom Hutchinson rampaged through Aldershot's midfield, fed Morgan, and he showed power and precision to hold off Anthony Straker and beat Bull.

It could have been worse for the Shots: Norville shot just wide and then, not for the first time, Charles let the ball bounce and Day hesitated. In nipped Goma Lambu, with just Bull to beat, but his finish was poor.

Minutes later, Gray took off Norville and the tide turned. It was Dixon, who had scarcely had a kick in the first 70 minutes, who made the real difference. His tenacity caught Danny Bunce, busy over-elaborating, unawares and a deft touch set Joel Grant clear. His cross-shot was parried by Gindre straight to Charles, who had remained in the area after a corner, and he gleefully smashed the ball into the roof of the net for his first goal of the season.

Three minutes later Dixon toed the ball away from Gindre after another corner, and the keeper crudely brought him down. John Grant kept his cool and swept the penalty home off the left post.

Woking never looked like equalising and Gray's body-language spoke volumes, as he slumped silently against the side of the dugout. In front of him, substitute Danny Hylton twisted past three challenges and the ball was sped to Joel Grant, who was fouled on the edge of the area. This was Aldershot at their best, with precise passes, made at pace, too quick in mind and movement for Woking's tiring players.

The Woking fans thought the Shots had wasted the set-piece but instead a clever move from Harding to Soares put in substitute Dean Smith. His shot was saved by Gindre but John Grant smashed home to make it 4-2.

John Grant, on his way to two late goals.

> **"**There was no need to panic when we were 2-1 down. We have scored late goals all season and I had a feeling we would do again today. It's a credit to our fitness levels. The FA Trophy is a fantastic competition. Winning is a habit and we want to keep on doing it.**"**
>
> Gary Waddock

ALDERSHOT TOWN 0

FOREST GREEN ROVERS 1

(Beesley 1)

19 January 2008

All good things must come to an end, and Forest Green Rovers proved it on Saturday, cutting down Aldershot's five-month strong winning run at the Rec.

But good things may yet come to those who wait, so, while this was a performance as disappointing as the result, the Shots remain six points clear at the top of Blue Square Premier. It is a handy position to be in towards the end of January. Fortress Rec has been sacked, but Gary Waddock's empire remains very much intact.

> *I've said all along that there will be twists and turns right to the end.*

"We were never going to win every game, but nor will the other teams involved at the top," said Waddock.

The race for the one automatic place to the Football League looks like being a three-horse race between the Shots, Stevenage Borough and Torquay United, although Burton Albion cannot be discounted either.

Good news for the Shots on Saturday was Torquay's 0-0 draw at Salisbury City and Cambridge United's continued poor form, but Peter Taylor's Stevenage, the busiest side in the January transfer window, are emerging as the biggest danger to Aldershot's ambitions.

Despite ten league wins in a row at home and 13 in all competitions, this result had been coming. Five months of winning is an outstanding achievement but recent league victories have all been narrow, with Woking and Rushden & Diamonds a little unfortunate and Stafford Rangers and Grays Athletic especially unlucky not to take something away from the Rec.

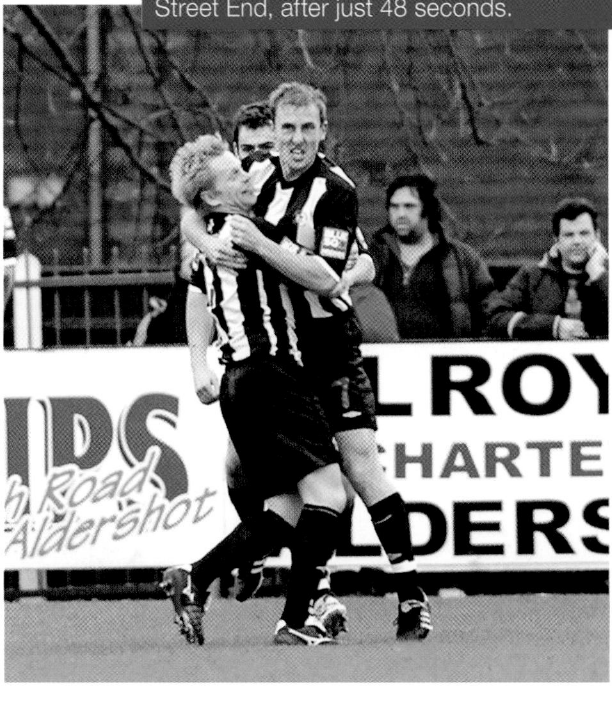

Beesley celebrates scoring at the High Street End, after just 48 seconds.

What has saved Aldershot until now is their goal-scoring prowess – you can score but we'll score more – but on Saturday it suffered a rare failure. The Shots lacked a killer instinct, dallying over opportunities and shooting too close to Rovers keeper Ryan Robinson on the too few times they tested him.

Without its goals, the attack could not carry a defence that creaks at the best of times but on Saturday was close to collapse, run ragged by the league's top scorer, Stuart Fleetwood, who looks set to leave for Crewe Alexandra or another League One side this week. Rhys Day, who still looked troubled by an achilles problem,

Danny Hylton is denied late on.

Anthony Charles and Dean Smith all endured torrid afternoons chasing Fleetwood's shadow.

Fleetwood's finishing was, for once, wayward but that was largely thanks to Aldershot keeper Nikki Bull, who did just enough on half a dozen occasions to narrow the angle or smother a shot.

Forest Green arrived less than an hour before kick-off, after traffic congestion, but it was the Shots who started at a crawl, handing Rovers the lead after just 48 seconds. Charles and Ricky Newman, playing in midfield with both Lewis Chalmers and Scott Davies suspended, hesitated on the edge of the area, allowing Alex Lawless to nip in and put Mark Beesley clear through, beating Bull with aplomb.

It could have been worse. In the first 15 minutes Day hacked down Anthony Tonkin on the edge of the area and Lawless' free kick was only inches over, Charles and Newman were rightly booked for late, uncontrolled tackles and Day and Smith, surprisingly picked in favour of Rob Gier, gave away possession repeatedly.

Only Ben Harding, once again the Shots' most consistent outfield player, and Anthony Straker, who did well attacking from left-back, looked likely to lift the Shots from their first half slumbers. Harding was inches wide with a dipping left-foot volley on 25 minutes and his curling free kick forced a fine save from Robinson seven minutes later.

With Kirk Hudson ill, Louie Soares started a league game for the first time since early December but lacked precision, taking too long to shoot after good work by Straker. Smith struggled at the back all game but he did at least look bright going forward, only to squander the Shots' best opportunity of the half by passing to Jonny Dixon when he should have shot.

Rovers got their tactics spot on in the second half, playing with the wind and launching long balls forward for Fleetwood's pace to exploit, although Aldershot played into their hands with a high backline that granted Fleetwood and Beesley, who were a far more threatening partnership than John Grant and Dixon, plenty of space to run into.

Day helped Fleetwood even further by inexplicably letting a ball fall over his head, straight to the striker, who bore down on goal. Bull did superbly well to force Fleetwood wide but Beesley still contrived to miss an open goal from Fleetwood's pass, hitting the post.

That extraordinary let-off lifted the crowd and a raucous atmosphere accompanied the rest of an absorbing half. Twice, Fleetwood skinned Day but hit the side netting, while Bull thwarted him after neat approach play from Beesley and the impressive Michael Brough.

Not that Aldershot didn't have their moments, with Joel Grant, who looked more dangerous as the game went on, having an effort cleared off the line, and Smith

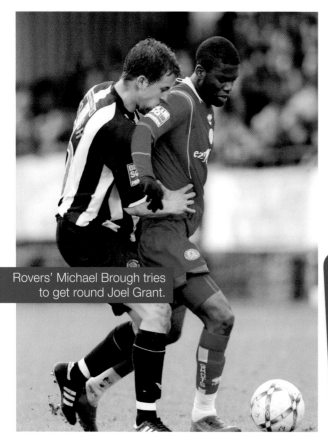

Rovers' Michael Brough tries to get round Joel Grant.

as an assistant to Howard Webb at this summer's European Championships, wasn't interested in any of that malarkey.

Bull made one further superb save, winning his personal joust with Fleetwood, even if his side lost the fight seconds later.

This match was actually a mere skirmish in a season-long war; Aldershot live to fight another day, from a position of strength. Fortress Rec has taken a beating but it is still standing strong. Moreover, four wins from the last five away games is impressive too. But while drawing a blank up front on Saturday was just a blip, the lack of pace at the back is an increasing cause for concern.

> "We didn't put in a performance and we didn't defend well. But we have had five months of winning at home and I certainly would have settled for that at the start of the season."
>
> Gary Waddock

forging forward, before shooting woefully wide.

Waddock went for broke, finishing the game with a 3-3-4 formation and fielding a bevy of attacking intent, adding Danny Hylton and Rob Elvins to the two Grants, Dixon and Soares. Perhaps it was too much as Harding, out-numbered in the middle, was less effective in the second half, blunted by Rovers' player-coach Jamie Pitman. Hylton, however, impressed in an all too brief 20-minute cameo, linking effectively with John Grant and creating two openings for himself, but Robinson thwarted him.

As the Shots grew more desperate, both John Grant and Hylton had hopeful penalty appeals turned down and captain Day was put out of his misery, replaced by Elvins. Rovers continued to defend in numbers and deserved their victory on that solid base alone, with excellent positioning, well-timed tackles and brave blocks simply too much for Aldershot, who ran out of steam and ideas.

Rovers should have added the gloss they merited in injury time. Fleetwood raced clear but fell under a tackle from behind by Smith in the area. Penalty – and surely a red card – was flagged by the assistant, but the referee Mullarkey surprised most in the ground by waving play on, indicating that Smith had got the ball.

Forest Green's management and substitutes ran onto the pitch to protest but Mullarkey, who will officiate

Forest Green's Simon Clist takes on Jonny Dixon.

DAYS THINKS IT ALL OVER

24 January 2008

Last Saturday against Forest Green was obviously a disappointing result and performance, and we had a long on-pitch meeting to talk things through at the start of training this week.

It's not just the Gaffer and Martin Kuhl who talk; everyone is allowed to have their say. It's a good idea to hear different opinions and we're confident we can rectify the mistakes we made. Obviously there was a lot of talk about Stuart Fleetwood before and after the game and I now know from personal experience that he's a very good player.

To be honest, I must put my hands up. I was guilty of not giving Fleetwood enough respect in the second half. As captain I was urging and pushing us forward, but in hindsight I should have sat back more and not allowed him so much space. It played into their hands. There's no hiding from the fact that Rovers were able to turn us far too easily at the back and then had masses of space to exploit.

Giero (Rob Gier) made an interesting point in the team meeting at training. Watching as a substitute from the side, he said it looked like we pushed forward much too early after the break, when we could have been more patient. We were only 1-0 down, after all, and we now realise that a better policy might have been to keep playing normally until the last 15 minutes, and only then laid siege to their goal.

But it's been a good week in training, and the lads are in good spirits. The Gaffer sent those of us not playing in Tuesday's reserves match on a really hard blow out on Tuesday morning, so we've been worked hard.

Charlesy (Anthony Charles) has, as usual, been the worst player at training. He always is. The other day the Gaffer absolutely skinned Charlesy in a five-a-side and put the ball through his legs. The Gaffer even shouted "nuts!" – he loved it. He and Martin like to get involved. You can still see that they've played at a very high level;

they've still got it, even if they do show their age when it comes to recovering from some of the fitness stuff!

Charlesy scored the best own-goal I've ever seen today too, a cracking volley. Thankfully he likes to save his proper performances for first team matches. He's suspended on Saturday at York and we will miss him at the back, but I'm confident whoever plays will do well.

We have a number of players back this weekend. It was good to see Scotty Davies, Lewis Chalmers and Kirk Hudson play for the reserves on Tuesday and we welcome them back. The competition for places is good, it keeps us all on our toes. Between now and the end of the season everyone will play their part.

I'm fighting fit after my achilles problem and raring to go for the York game on Saturday. I'm on four bookings, so I'm aware I'm one tackle away from a ban but that's what happens at this time of the season. You have to forget about it and play your normal game. Strakes (Anthony Straker) is in the same boat.

I didn't play at York last season, I was injured, but I did play there when I was with Mansfield Town. We won 2-1 (February 2004) and my main memory is that the pitch was diabolical. With all the rain around, we've been training on some pretty poor pitches recently, so at least that will stand us in good stead for Saturday's match.

Talking of Mansfield, I still have plenty of friends at the club and I'll be looking out for their result tomorrow against Middlesbrough in the FA Cup fourth round. I enjoyed my time at Mansfield and don't like seeing them struggling at the bottom of the Football League, so it's good they have a big cup tie tomorrow.

But obviously the big game for us tomorrow is our trip to York. We were never going to win every game but we understand the importance of bouncing back with a win after losing to Forest Green. York will be tough opponents but it doesn't matter who the Gaffer picks, we all believe we can get back to winning ways.

YORK CITY 2

(Brodie 7, Woolford 86)

26 January 2008

ALDERSHOT TOWN 0

LINE-UP

Bull, Smith, Straker, Winfield, Day, Chalmers, Soares, Davies (Joel Grant 62), John Grant, Dixon (Hylton 65), Harding.

The Yorkies had their cake generously handed to them on a plate by Aldershot Town at KitKat Crescent on Saturday and ate it with relish.

Such was York's dominance that the 2-0 score flattered Aldershot, who looked anything but league leaders, run ragged at the back, out-fought and out-thought in midfield and devoid of any thrust in attack. It was the Minstermen against the Mr Men and, sadly for Aldershot, it was Messrs Slow, Clumsy, Muddle and Forgetful clad in the Shots' dark blue.

This was the first time this season that the Shots have failed to bounce back from defeat with a win and, while they are still top of Blue Square Premier, their lead over Torquay United and Stevenage Borough is now fragile.

In fairness, it is almost unheard of in football for a team to cruise through a season, and the Shots' travails are no different to the malaise currently suffered by League Two leaders MK Dons, or Watford in the Championship. The key is how quickly Gary Waddock can reinvigorate his side and he was eager to accentuate the positive after the defeat.

> **" We were always likely to have a little period when things don't quite go our way. "**

"There's nothing we can do about that now. We don't dwell on wins and we won't dwell on days like this. The guys are disappointed but are in a very positive frame of mind. We will turn this around, we know what we need to do. There is no panic."

But Aldershot must improve fast, with Oxford United visiting the Recreation Ground on Tuesday. They were second-best in every department on Saturday. York passed and moved the ball superbly but were stronger in the tackle too and by far the more industrious. And

Aldershot simply never got to grips with York's 3-5-2 formation.

The Shots' defence has looked fragile all season and no one should have been too surprised that it was stretched by a side unbeaten in 12 games and fresh from thrashing Grays Athletic 4-1 in the FA Trophy. York are on the rise, just like the flood water of the city's River Ouse this week. Northern uprisings have been ruthlessly put down from the south before, however. Granted, Henry VIII's spate of executions and imposition of martial law after the York-based Pilgrimage of Grace uprising in 1536 would perhaps have been taking things a little too far but Waddock knew his side would have to stand up and be counted. But they failed to do so.

Aldershot were without the suspended Anthony Charles, their best defender, and Waddock surprisingly favoured Dean Smith and David Winfield ahead of Rob Gier and Ricky Newman. Smith was especially poor at right back and captain Rhys Day would have benefited from Newman's assurance and good positional sense alongside him in the middle. Anthony Straker, at left back, celebrated his call-up to the Barbados squad with his worst performance for several weeks. The Shots were simply too weedy to cope with York's blooming White Rose.

Aldershot's march to the top had been buoyed by a glut of goals and the ability to steal narrow victories. But the Shots offered next to nothing going forward on Saturday, and never looked like equalising, despite trailing by just the one goal for as long as 79 minutes.

Waddock chose to field his most powerful midfield — Ben Harding, Lewis Chalmers, Scott Davies and Louie Soares — but that was at the expense of the side's creativity. Granted, he could do nothing about Kirk Hudson's thigh injury, but accommodating Davies, back from a four-game ban, meant sacrificing the invention and unpredictability of Joel Grant and moving

Harding away from the middle, where he has become so influential.

Davies and Chalmers were no match for York's tireless central trio of Stuart Elliott, Nicky Wroe and the outstanding Emmanuel Panther, a big cat against Aldershot's kittens. No Aldershot player was allowed any time to settle on the ball, and wing-backs Anthony Lloyd and Simon Rusk were able to enjoy the freedom of the flanks.

"I know that Ben Harding's best position is in the middle but by starting him on the left I was still picking the team that I thought gave us the best chance of winning the game," said Waddock.

Aldershot did, in fact, start brightly and penned York in their own half for the first few minutes. Chalmers even mustered a weak shot on target. But, after that, York keeper Tom Evans could have taken the afternoon off.

Day and Straker left 'Angel of the North' Richard Brodie completely unmarked to head in Wroe's seventh-minute cross. Nikki Bull, rooted to his line, should perhaps have done better too but at least he kept the score at 1-0, diving bravely at the feet of Martyn Woolford, whose movement was too much for Day and Winfield.

The only glimmer of hope for the Shots was a shocking tackle by Darren Craddock on John Grant, but referee Malader handed out just a yellow card. Besides, it was hard to imagine Aldershot being any more creative against ten men than they were against 11.

After the break Aldershot were marginally better and enjoyed plenty of possession, but their intricate passing was all too easily broken up by centre-back David McKurk. With York sitting deep, the Shots could not get in behind and on the one occasion Soares did launch a promising raid, there was no one to support him. Then again his set-piece delivery was desperately poor all afternoon.

With every break York looked likely to extend their advantage. Lloyd and Wroe, set up by Panther, both shot just wide, before Bull got all four fingers (well, it was at the KitKat Crescent!) to turn aside Woolford's stinging shot. York should have been out of sight but showed no signs of fretting over their profligacy. Four minutes from time their win was duly sealed after Day misjudged Panther's lobbed pass and substitute Craig Farrell crossed for Woolford to sweep past Bull.

While York had their cake and ate it, Aldershot lacked the hunger even to scrap for the scraps, starving the few hundred Shots fans who made the journey of any cheer. At least, for now, the Blue Square Premier table remains a considerable crumb of comfort but the side must regain their appetite for the fight against Oxford.

> **Basic errors have cost us in the last two games. But we won't dwell on defeat, just as we don't dwell on wins. The squad is in a positive frame of mind. We will turn this around and come good again. There is no need to panic.**
>
> Gary Waddock

ALDERSHOT TOWN 1
(John Grant 65)

OXFORD UNITED 0

29 January 2008

Character was what Gary Waddock had demanded from his players before this vital match and they didn't let him down, forcing a 1-0 win more through great desire than grand design.

The pressure was on after two league losses and Aldershot proved that they have the mental and physical strength to bounce back.

It was certainly not the prettiest of Aldershot's 11 wins in 12 Blue Square Premier matches at the Recreation Ground, but it was probably the most important, after those two defeats had seen the Shots' lead shrink at the top of the table, with Torquay United and Stevenage closing in. Now the lead is back to six points and while Torquay have two games in hand, the pressure is now on them to respond.

Aldershot rode their luck. Rob Gier, reinstated at right-back in place of Dean Smith, was fortunate not to concede a penalty for a challenge on Justin Richards in the first minute, Oxford's Matty Day rattled the bar in the last ten minutes with a scorching shot and, before Grant's goal, the U's' spoiling tactics and nasty niggles had briefly looked like strangling the game.

But this was a deserved victory, inspired by hard, steely work and crowned by a purple patch in the second half, in which Grant nodded home the winner from Louie Soares' corner in the 65th minute. It was Grant's 15th league goal of the season, but his first since a hat-trick at Salisbury in early December.

Languid and limited at York, the Shots were powerful and pacy in this match, even if they rarely rediscovered their true fluency, against opponents who are in transition and the middle of a woeful run. For the dreaming spires of Oxford, this season has been a nightmare.

But the Shots were vastly improved from Saturday. Anthony Charles, back from suspension, dominated the defence, Ben Harding and Lewis Chalmers, rightly reunited in the centre of midfield, bit into tackles and moved the ball quickly and intelligently, and Joel Grant added the flair, if not the finish.

Two home-grown talents, Danny Hylton and Dave Winfield, were highly impressive too. Hylton was only starting due to Jonny Dixon's imminent move to Brighton & Hove Albion, while Winfield kept his place after the York debacle, preferred in place of captain Rhys Day, who was dropped to the bench.

That was a brave decision by Waddock and Winfield justified his manager's faith with a performance that grew in stature, crowned by two superb tackles in succession on Oxford's Yemi Odubade, who impressed as a substitute as Oxford changed formation to 4-4-3 after Grant's goal.

Hylton had a quiet first half but was inspirational afterwards and lit the spark that carried Aldershot to victory, with a swivel and peach of a half-volley that

John Grant scrambles the winner before leading the celebrations (opposite).

Aldershot had forced the issue and gained their reward. They made a mess of things at York but in this match they made things happen, which is how to win games when you are still not at your best. No wonder Waddock was so pleased with his young side at the final whistle.

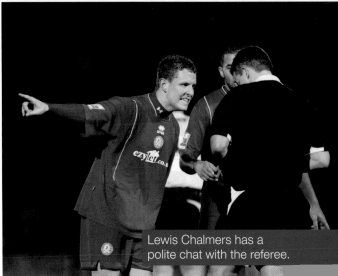

Lewis Chalmers has a polite chat with the referee.

flew inches wide soon after the break. The East Bank responded by raising the decibels and the players raised their game.

Waddock was especially vocal from the touchline, cajoling some players and challenging others to maintain a high tempo and never give Oxford a rest. "Move the ball," and "Take him on," repeated Waddock throughout the game, forcing chances to come if his side couldn't craft them.

It was a sound tactic on the back of two games without a goal but when the chances fell in the first half, John Grant had a header blocked and shot tamely when put through by namesake Joel. Harding and Soares were both wasteful from presentable set-pieces and the half petered out.

But the longer the game went on, the more purposeful the Shots became. Fittingly, when the goal arrived, it was more beast than beauty, bundled home in a crowded area off John Grant's head and more. But it had been instigated by superb defending from Charles and Winfield a minute before and the Shots had swept forward with pace, unnerving Oxford into conceding an unnecessary corner.

> "The biggest thing for me tonight was the character we showed. People outside the club were looking at us and saying that after two defeats on the trot our bubble had burst, we were in a crisis. Well, if that's a crisis, long may it continue, if the players perform under pressure like they did today.
>
> Make no mistake, this was a big win for us and it was a delighted dressing room after the game. Recent performances have not been at the level we demand but tonight's level of performance was pleasing."
>
> Gary Waddock

DIXON DEPARTS

It was goodbye to a fans' favourite this week as Aldershot Town striker Jonny Dixon sealed a surprise switch to League One side Brighton & Hove Albion.

Dixon played for the Shots in three spells, twice on loan from Wycombe Wanderers (in seasons 2004/05 and 2005/06) before the Shots' faithful helped then manager Terry Brown buy Dixon for £6,000 just over a year ago. In all, Dixon scored 26 Nationwide Conference goals for Aldershot and three in the FA Cup.

"It was only thanks to the Aldershot fans that I came back to the Rec," said Dixon, speaking after his move to Brighton. "They are simply the best fans I have ever played in front of and are just fantastic. I couldn't have asked for more from them, they were great to me from the very start.

"I hope I entertained them in my spells with the club and maybe I'll come back to the Rec in some capacity one day."

Dixon admits he is 'very excited to be back in the Football League' but is sad to be leaving Aldershot, especially with the club pushing hard for promotion to the League.

"I am disappointed to be going after working so hard with the guys to get Aldershot into such a good position," said Dixon. There have been plenty of unsubstantiated rumours linking Shots keeper Nikki Bull with a move to Brighton, but Dixon's move came completely out of the blue.

"It really came as a shock to me. I was having dinner on Monday evening and the phone rang and things went from there. I would happily have turned down a League Two club but I just couldn't say no to a League One side like Brighton," said the 24-year-old.

"I didn't get to see many of the Aldershot lads as I wasn't at Tuesday's training but I have spoken to most of the guys on the phone since then. I've made some really good, close friends at Aldershot and I will miss people. I liked everyone. I sat near Rhys [Day], Granty [John Grant] and Charlesy [Anthony Charles] in the dressing room, so it will be odd to be in one without them there.

"And then there were the guys I was a very similar age to, like Ben Harding and Giero [Rob Gier], who I got on really well with. But that's football. Players move from club to club and things change. I've already trained with the Brighton guys and the atmosphere seems to be good. They are a young bunch too, like at Aldershot."

Dixon has many happy memories of scoring for the Shots, especially during his first spell when his nine goals from 12 starts - and distinctive dreadlocks - endeared him to the faithful.

"My first goals for the club were special. It was my first ever FA Cup game and we beat Canvey Island 4-0 and I got two, including one from 30 yards. Aaron Mclean got the other two.

"The hat-trick I got in the league win at Gravesend & Northfleet that season was great for me too, and my last game before I was recalled by Wycombe.

"It was always good to score against the so-called big teams at that level too, such as Barnet. I got a couple against them when they were flying at the top of the table. But sometimes it's the simple ones, like the very late header from two yards against Grays Athletic last season. I enjoyed that winner."

Dixon scored again against Grays this season, home and away, but little did he know when he scored a consolation goal in Essex on 29 December that it would be his last goal for Aldershot. But he still made a significant contribution to the Shots' season after that, in the FA Trophy at Woking last month, winning possession and a penalty through sheer hard work, providing goals for Charles and John Grant and turning the game on its head.

There have been some exemplary finishes this season – notably at Crawley Town and Cambridge United in the FA Cup and Weymouth in the league – but for the rest of this season Aldershot may miss Dixon's ceaseless work and clever linking with the midfield, just as much as his goals.

But many of the best memories are from that first loan spell three seasons ago, when the goals flowed as the Shots' dreadlocked hero gave them a new cutting edge.

DAYS THINKS IT ALL OVER

31 January 2008

We have said goodbye to JD (Jonny Dixon) this week and we are all sad to see him leave.

We will all miss him and not just on the park. Jonny was one of the lads, a lovely bloke. No one ever had a bad word to say about him. But we are all really pleased for him. It's a great opportunity to join Brighton in League One and he couldn't really turn it down.

Everyone is aware during the transfer window that something might come up. Jonny is just one of many in the squad who might have attracted interest from League clubs, after the way we've been playing this season.

I think Jonny was as surprised as anyone. The phone call to the club from Brighton was out of the blue. The first we knew something might be happening was at training on Tuesday. Everyone was asking: "Why isn't JD here?"

But I didn't get full wind of it until after the Oxford game. I spoke to JD on Wednesday and wished him well. He said he was sad to be leaving us in such a good spot but I think everyone involved thought it was a good offer for all concerned.

I was dropped to the bench for that Oxford game. In my last two starts (Forest Green Rovers and York City) I was simply not up to scratch and I was very disappointed with myself. To be honest, I could see the decision to drop me coming. It was affecting me in training and the Gaffer could sense something was up with me and called me in to have a chat. We agreed that I haven't been playing too well and the Gaffer said he was going to make a change, just to keep me and the rest of the guys on their toes.

It was typical of the Gaffer to speak to me first, alone, so I knew before everyone else. I was pleased about that and respect him for it. Besides, we know that we have a squad of 18-20 players, rather than just an XI, and if we are going to win the Blue Square Premier then all of us will be needed in the next few months.

I've known some players who sulk after getting dropped but you won't be getting anything like that from me. I'm determined to win my place back and I said to the Gaffer that I'm going to get back in the team and make sure that he never drops me again.

I thought Charlesy and Dave Winfield were outstanding in the win over Oxford. Dave was fantastic. He kept his place ahead of me and I take my hat off to him. He had a great game. I was thrilled for us to get that win and a clean sheet. You always try and put results behind you but I think we could all sense that we were a bit uptight in training after the two defeats. But the whole place has been lifted by that Oxford win. It was a very important one, against a side who I thought weren't bad at all, and there is a brilliant feeling back in the squad.

We now turn to the FA Trophy match against Braintree. Obviously there will be no JD and Kirk Hudson was only due to return to training on Friday, so we may still be without him.

We have a couple of 'international stars' in the squad, of course, now that both Soaresy [Louie Soares] and Strakes [Anthony Straker] have been called up by Barbados.

Then again, perhaps that's going a bit too far, I think it's fair to say that Barbados is not exactly the greatest footballing nation in the world! Still, it's very good news for them, even if we're still not sure when we'll be losing them for a game or two. They are meant to go next week but have still not been given any itinerary by the Barbados footballing authorities. They say that everything and everyone is laid back in the Caribbean and clearly football is no exception.

Soaresy and I joined the Gaffer for one of our local promotions at Specsavers in Aldershot on Thursday. It was a good laugh, actually, trying on lots of different glasses and we got some good pictures. It's good to raise the profile of the club and set up sponsorship deals. Hopefully we can continue to raise the profile of the club on the pitch too, starting against Braintree.

ALDERSHOT TOWN 3

(John Grant 17, 85, Harding 52)

BRAINTREE TOWN 0

2 February 2008
FA Trophy

Watching your team play at Wembley should be a dream come true for all football fans, but this May's potential fixtures at the home of football leave the Aldershot faithful in a quandary.

One May day fixture at Wembley could be a last resort: the Conference play-off final, should the remainder of the league season not go to plan. Another is the FA Trophy final, that Shots fans would surely savour. But then again, not if through injuries, suspensions or sheer exhaustion, the Trophy costs the club that vital promotion which is the season's priority.

So, the Trophy is a little lost in no man's land, a fact illustrated by the thin turn-out of 1,772 to watch Aldershot see off Conference South Braintree Town 3-0 and ease into the last eight of the Trophy. Winning matches in the Trophy remains a good thing; Saturday's 3rd round win did, after all, warm the Aldershot coffers with £6,000 worth of prize money.

But Louie Soares also limped off with an injury and is a doubt for Saturday's league game at Farsley Celtic and Lewis Chalmers picked up another booking. Indeed, another referee might have sent off both him and Anthony Charles, which could have caused very real damage to the promotion bid.

The Aldershot players were certainly distracted in the first half, although they were still too good for a Braintree side who showed little ability and seemed unwilling to harass opponents who are, after all, top of the non-league pyramid. This surely was Braintree's 'cup final' and Aldershot would not have fancied a trip to Essex for a replay.

Eventually, after the break, Braintree did raise their game – and the temperature of the match, with a feisty attitude, to put it mildly – before the Shots' superior play and fitness saw them to a comfortable 3-0 victory, with Ben Harding's 25-yard thunderbolt the highlight of the game, sandwiched by a goal in either half by John Grant.

By selecting the strongest side available to him, Waddock made it clear that he's in top gear on the road to Wembley, even if his players coasted along in third at times.

A number of the Blue Square Premier's top clubs remain in the competition too, including Torquay United and Burton Albion, as well as in-form York. So, tougher opponents than Braintree may lie ahead.

But a side can only beat what is put in front of it and Aldershot completely controlled the first half once Grant had given them the lead, scuffing a shot in off the inside of the far post after Danny Hylton had dummied Chalmers' through ball.

The Shots should have scored more, with Hylton forcing a good save from Nicky Morgan, Anthony Straker narrowly missing with a cross-shot and Harding deflecting John Grant's cross wide of a gaping goal.

Charles was immaculate and completely dominant at the back and captain Rhys Day, recalled in place of

John Grant scores.

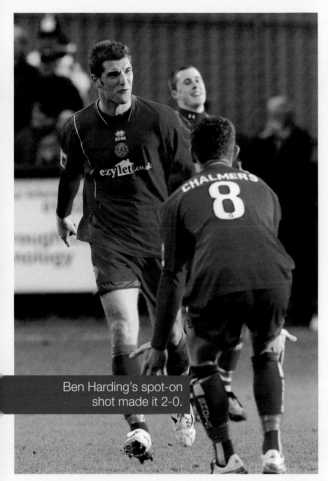

Ben Harding's spot-on shot made it 2-0.

a right-footed 25-yard screamer, in off the underside of the bar, to make it 2-0. Not that the woodwork's work was done as two minutes later Sullivan hit the junction of bar and post with a rising left-foot shot, with Bull well beaten.

After those frenzied three minutes, tempers flared, with Chalmers booked for a dangerous tackle and Baker and Quinton taking exception to Charles' defence of his midfield colleague.

While the Aldershot players were no saints, Quinton's theatrics were especially unnecessary, in embarrassing bouts of argy-bargy, with the Braintree captain seldom far from the epicentre. Thankfully, once Charles was booked for a silly late tackle the game calmed down and Aldershot ran away with possession and might easily have scored more than just the one late goal.

Scott Davies, who had a bright game after replacing Soares in the 34th minute, should have shot but instead over-elaborated in trying to set up a tap-in for Chalmers. Harding had a left-footed effort well saved and then substitute Kirk Hudson, making a welcome return from injury, forced Morgan into another good save, after a mesmerising run by Hylton.

Waddock withdrew Hylton with ten minutes to go, bringing on Rob Elvins, and Hylton was given a rousing reception by the Recreation Ground crowd. If Hylton can add goals to his hard-work and clever play, then Jonny Dixon will not be missed.

No-one needs a goal more than Elvins and he missed a good late opportunity, but was also instrumental in moves setting up two simple chances for John Grant. The first he missed before he slid in Davies' cross in the 85th minute, by which time even Quinton had been silenced.

Dave Winfield, who had a neck injury, looked very solid. The only disappointment was Dean Smith, who, with Rob Gier hampered with a hamstring injury, was given another chance at right-back, but continued to struggle for form after his autumn injury.

To be fair to Braintree, they started the second half superbly, with Chris Sullivan, who came on at the restart, adding desperately needed pace up front alongside James Baker and Bradley Quinton, their talented but tiresome captain, who spent much of the half squabbling rather than playing football.

Inside the first two minutes both Quinton and Adrian Deane failed to trouble Nikki Bull after beating the offside trap, as the Shots, not for the first time, started a half sluggishly.

But Aldershot did emerge from their slumbers and two classy moments illustrated the gulf in class between the two teams.

First, Hylton was desperately unlucky when a first-time lob from distance scraped the outside of the post, after Morgan was stranded after tackling John Grant on the edge of his area.

Seconds later Harding, whose game just seems to get better and better, was inches more accurate, cracking

> "The object was simple: to get through. And we have done that. It was a professional performance. We perhaps weren't at our best but we kept a clean sheet and scored three goals, so we are happy."
>
> Gary Waddock

ST ALBANS CITY 0

ALDERSHOT TOWN 4

(Hudson 4, Elvins 19, 45, Donnelly 75)

5 February 2008
Setanta Shield

LINE-UP

Jaimez-Ruiz, Smith, Milletti, Day, Koo-Boothe, Newman (Hylton 70), Donnelly, Davies, Elvins, Hudson, Joel Grant (Straker 76).

Playing on Shrove Tuesday evening may have deprived Aldershot Town of pancakes but they at least had the satisfaction of battering St Albans City.

This was a victory even more comfortable than the 4-0 score suggests. City, struggling in Conference South, had no answer to Aldershot's pace – Kirk Hudson's especially – passing and set-pieces in the first half and at the break the home side were already 3-0 down. The contest was over.

The Romans ruthlessly struck down St Alban – Britain's first Christian martyr – in the third century AD and this was little different: Gary Waddock's soldiers were uncompromising, professional and deadly too. And they march on in yet another competition.

The fixture congestion is mounting for Aldershot, but the flip side is that the Setanta Shield provides Gary Waddock with competitive games in which to blood fringe players and ease back key men from injury.

Tuesday's team may have included just three starters from Saturday's 3-0 FA Trophy win over Braintree – Dean Smith, Rhys Day and Joel Grant (Waddock named a very strong bench to stay within the competition rules) – but it was nonetheless a hungry side and one laced with first-team experience. Ricky Newman and Scott Davies also started.

The goalscorers alone provided Waddock with plenty of cheer: one from Hudson, who played the full 90 minutes and will be pushing for a start in the league tomorrow at Farsley Celtic, either up front or out wide; a rare brace from striker Rob Elvins; and a magnificent 25-yard strike from Scott Donnelly, in his most significant game for the club so far.

Elvins has long since lost his starting place in the Blue Square Premier and, even with Jonny Dixon sold to Brighton, he currently plays second fiddle to Danny Hylton and Hudson too, should Waddock consider the latter as a striker. But Waddock believes in the man he brought in from West Bromwich Albion in the summer.

> **I'm delighted for Rob that he got two goals.**
>
> Gary Waddock

Elvins' strikes hardly set the world alight, first tapping into an empty net after a disastrous misunderstanding between St Albans' Ben Martin and keeper Nick Eyre after 19 minutes – although credit to Elvins for putting them under pressure – and then bundling home Scott Davies' corner from a few yards out on the stroke of half-time. That goal was in virtually identical fashion to Hudson's third minute goal and Davies' deadball delivery caused the home side problems all evening.

But Elvins had been unlucky earlier with a towering header that flew just over the bar and was neat and tidy throughout. With the squad as it is now, if John Grant gets injured or suspended, then Waddock might need Elvins' physical presence up front. The more confident he is, the better.

Donnelly's goal, in the 75th minute, completely eclipsed the game's previous strikes and was probably even better than Ben Harding's scorcher against Braintree three days before. But the 20-year-old, who is at

Aldershot after failing to make the grade at Queens Park Rangers, largely due to injury, had already caught the eye with some inventive long-range passing.

Elsewhere, Jason Milletti slotted in tidily at left back and Nathan Koo-Boothe started at centre-back, alongside Day. Both players were solid, although St Albans' Bradley Gray, Hassan Sulaiman and substitute Jomo Faal-Thomas caused the odd uncomfortable moment for both of them, as well as Mikhael Jaimez-Ruiz in goal. Koo-Boothe grew in stature as the game progressed, however, and his distribution from the back after the break was impressive.

> **" Nathan [Koo-Boothe] needs to bed down in the squad and get games under his belt. But he did well and it's nice to have competition for places. "**
>
> Gary Waddock

The second half was anything but competitive but, with a win, no cards and no serious injuries, that suited Aldershot perfectly. Hopes for the Conference, FA Trophy and Setanta Shield treble are still alive.

DAYS THINKS IT ALL OVER

7 February 2008

We had a good training session on Thursday morning. It was pretty hard, to be honest, but Thursday to Saturday gives plenty of time to rest, as we'll just have a shorter session on Friday.

Charlesy (Anthony Charles) was up to his usual tricks. We often play a game of two-touch 'keepy-uppy' and Charlesy is the worst player I have ever seen at it. He also has a habit in training of trying to kick the ball as hard as possible at players, for no reason, which is nice. (Indeed, fans watching Aldershot warm up at St Albans on Tuesday evening will have seen Charles repeatedly welly the ball at teammates when they weren't watching.)

Obviously we have a very busy week or so coming up in the league, with Farsley on Saturday and home matches against Cambridge and Stevenage quickly after that. But all we can do is concentrate on Farsley. It's another long trip and we're hoping we won't have the coach journey we had up to York, which took about six hours. We will train on Friday morning at 10am, have lunch together back at the Rec and then head off to stay overnight in a hotel near Farsley.

Surprise, surprise, I will be rooming with Charlesy. Actually, he's not too bad at all as roommates go. He keeps quiet and will happily just put on his earphones and watch his portable DVD player. I'm told that Lewis Chalmers is the roommate to avoid. We've all seen him moan at referees but apparently he moans all the time off the pitch too: "The room's too cold, the room's now too hot, there aren't enough towels," that sort of thing.

We were all quite pleased with our performances against Braintree and St Albans. They were two good cup wins, even if the opposition were from the league below. Dave Winfield's neck injury gave me an early chance back in the team after losing my place. I was ready to take my chance but I must admit that I thought I might be out of the team for while, as Dave and the rest of the defence had done really well without me against Oxford United. I'm pleased with the way things went; two clean sheets and seven goals were a good return for the team.

Everyone was really happy that Rob Elvins scored a couple of goals at St Albans. I was willing him forward to go and get that hat-trick. I thought he did really well for the first goal, going in bravely with their big defender and forcing the error.

It was good to see Kirk Hudson back too. He couldn't make training on Thursday but will back on Friday. I don't know whether he'll start on Saturday but even if he's just on the bench, it's a massive boost to have him. Having him to bring on will really scare defenders. Danny Hylton's done well since Jonny Dixon left too. Danny's a good player, with bags of talent and a good work ethic. He just needs to believe in himself and I think we're starting to see that.

We have lots of fixtures coming up and we'll need the whole squad to contribute. We are still in four competitions and believe we can win them all. If we win the Blue Square Premier, FA Trophy, Setanta Shield and Hampshire Cup, then surely we'll have a good chance of winning the BBC Sports Team of the Year award in December. Well, that's my aim, anyway!

We have a few get-togethers as a team away from football. Paintballing before Christmas was great fun and the Gaffer was due to organise a clay pigeon shooting day recently but we had to cancel that as we have so many games. Maybe once things calm down we might have time to go go-karting or something like that.

We always eat together after training, which is good for team bonding. I guess that sounds a bit like the new England set-up. But the Gaffer hasn't started calling us by our surnames or anything like that. Actually, I wouldn't really want to repeat what he calls some players on some occasions. But I think it's fair to say that he's not as strict as England's Mr Capello.

Anyway, it's time to turn to Farsley now. Hopefully a good number of fans will make the trip north and we can reward them with a win.

9 February 2008

FARSLEY CELTIC 1
(Reeves 70)

ALDERSHOT TOWN 3
(Hylton 32, Hudson 62, 90)

LINE-UP

Bull, Gier (Day 81), Straker, Winfield, Charles, Chalmers, Hudson, Harding, John Grant, Hylton (Elvins 90), Joel Grant (Newman 64).

Goals from two of Aldershot Town's highly promising young guns secured a tenth away win of the season, with Danny Hylton's first league goal confirming there is life after Jonny Dixon.

The home side were quickest into their stride, although for all the early possession, Farsley offered little threat to the Shots' goal. Indeed it was Aldershot who had the first real attempt, when Hudson unleashed a 20-yard thunderbolt that Celtic keeper Curtis Aspden could only push to John Grant, whose shot from a narrow angle was cleared off the line by Matt Jackson.

Hudson's flair and pace caused plenty of trouble for the home team, and he was not afraid to have a go from long range either, much like Hylton, whose 25-yard shot on target was deflected for a corner.

It was from that Harding corner that Hylton opened the scoring on 32 minutes with a glancing header from the edge of the six-yard box that prompted gleeful celebrations befitting a first league goal of his fledgling Shots career.

There were opportunities for Aldershot to extend their lead before the break. When Rob Gier had played the ball in, John Grant looked certain to score a headed goal into the top right-hand corner but Aspden appeared from nowhere to touch the ball over the bar. Anthony Charles also missed narrowly when he slid in at the far post, while Grant did well to work some space for himself in the box only to see his delicate chip float agonisingly wide of the post.

It was more of the same after the break, with Aldershot's slick attacking play putting the home defence on the backfoot. Hudson went on a pacey run to the edge of the Farsley box, playing in Grant, whose shot from eight yards bobbled just wide of the post with the keeper beaten.

Within a minute, Grant was in with a scoring chance once again. The combative Lewis Chalmers turned provider with a nicely weighted pass that put the goal in sight, but his on-target effort forced a good save from the busy Aspden.

At this point you could have been forgiven for thinking the all-important second goal was not going to come for Aldershot, but then Hylton and Harding combined quickly and efficiently to carve out an opening for Hudson, who made no mistake, putting the ball in the net from the right-hand side of the area on 62 minutes.

With the Shots looking comfortable in everything they did, it seemed there was no way they would rue a missed chance by Hylton a few minutes later. However, on 70 minutes an error by Charles, who had been a towering influence in defence all afternoon, opened the door for the home side who are scrapping for every point in their fight against relegation.

All of a sudden it was game on at 2-1, with 20 minutes still to play. Farsley piled men forward, and a touch from experienced substitute Steve Torpey found fellow sub James Knowles, whose crashing shot from less than ten yards hit the underside of the bar with Bull stranded.

The game was getting frantic, so much so that Hylton, who was giving George Santos a tough afternoon, became the fourth Shots player to be shown a yellow card, joining Charles, Winfield and Joel Grant in the referee's notebook.

However, it was Aldershot who put the five minutes of extra time to best use, as John Grant and substitute Ricky Newman combined well down the left. It was an excellent ball from Newman that gave Hudson his second goal of the game, three minutes into the added time, with a finish that was almost a carbon copy of his cool finish earlier in the half.

ALDERSHOT TOWN 0

CAMBRIDGE UNITED 0

LINE-UP

Bull, Gier, Winfield, Charles, Straker, Hudson, Joel Grant (Day 83), Chalmers, Harding, Elvins (Davies 61), John Grant.

In most cases, being held at home by a fellow promotion rival looks like two points dropped. But it was more like a point gained for Aldershot Town on Tuesday night as they played out an entertaining 0-0 draw with sixth place Cambridge United at the Rec.

Not only did the Shots keep a 13-point advantage over their opponents but, as Torquay were unexpectedly held at lowly Weymouth, it was clearly Aldershot's night, especially as they survived with ten men after Anthony Charles was sent off. Even local rivals Woking did the Shots a favour, halting Exeter's sudden rise with a last-gasp equaliser. Well, what are neighbours for?

Aldershot made a bright start to the game and Ben Harding curled in a free kick that Cambridge keeper Danny Potter gathered with ease. Two minutes later and Charles picked up his first booking, after a challenge with Dan Gleeson.

The game quickly became a scrappy affair, as the Shots in particular were guilty of bypassing the midfield. A defence as mean as Cambridge's had little trouble dealing with that, and it was the visitors who came closest to breaking the deadlock on 27 minutes when Nikki Bull's spilled ball was shot over the bar by Lee McEvilly.

It was Cambridge who looked the more lively, and when ex-Chelsea trainee Rob Wolleaston got in down the left and cut a low ball across the face of the area, Scott Rendell just failed to touch it home as he slid in at the back post. The Shots did briefly threaten when Joel Grant played a neat one-two with Lewis Chalmers, but his cross couldn't pick out either John Grant or Elvins.

After the break, Aldershot made a more purposeful start to the half, but Cambridge were still a danger at the other end, and should have scored just before the hour. Courtney Pitt skipped past Rob Gier and lifted a perfect cross to the back post for the arriving Mark Beesley. The midfielder struck a sweet volley towards goal but Bull was equal to it, saving low to his left.

Waddock decided it was time for a change and withdrew an ineffectual Elvins for Davies, moving Hudson up front. It had an almost immediate effect and the Shots had more cutting edge up front as Hudson came to the fore.

The young striker lashed a viciously swerving 25-yard strike at goal moments later, and somehow Potter turned it around the post with a superb save.

On 66 minutes came the Shots' best chance of the game when Hudson broke in the middle of the park, picking out Davies. The on-loan Reading youngster knocked a first-time ball into John Grant's path, sending him through on goal.

But the 17-goal striker is not in the same rich vein of form that he showed at the start of the campaign, and he took an age to line up his shot before firing tamely at Potter.

On 81 minutes, Charles picked up his second yellow, adjudged to have deliberately handballed a pass that would have set Lee Boylan free. It could have been a pivotal moment in the game, as Rhys Day came on for Joel Grant in an attempt to plug the gap, but in fact the Shots seemed to step up their search for the winner.

Davies had a good impact on the game and in the 90th minute he sent Hudson through down the right. Hudson's pace saw him race clear, but with Grant square of him in the area, he shot into the side netting.

Then in stoppage time an even better chance came Aldershot's way. Davies split the defence to send John Grant clean through again. With more composure he would have won it, but shot straight at a relieved Potter and the sides settled for a hard-earned point.

ALDERSHOT TOWN 3
(Joel Grant 9, John Grant 18 pen, Hylton 30)

STEVENAGE BOROUGH 1
(Gavin Grant 63)

An almost perfect first half display spectacularly put paid to any claims that Aldershot cannot beat the other top teams in the Blue Square Premier.

This was Aldershot's sixth game against one of the quartet chasing the league leaders hardest – Torquay United, Cambridge United, Burton Albion and Stevenage Borough – and their first win, after two draws against Cambridge and defeats against the other three.

Stevenage's lumbering defence and lacklustre midfield had no answer to Aldershot's marauding front four, with Joel Grant and Kirk Hudson explosive down the flanks, Danny Hylton a bag of tricks in the middle and John Grant a powerful leader of the attack.

But all over the pitch Aldershot were superior: fullbacks Rob Gier and Anthony Straker were able to play as supplementary wingers, Ben Harding and Lewis Chalmers had total control of the midfield and Dave Winfield and Rhys Day, back in as captain for the

John Grant scored a second for the Shots.

suspended Anthony Charles, were rock solid. Stevenage had no answer; their beleagured, shell-shocked players looked to Peter Taylor for guidance but he was too busy exploding on the touchline.

Little wonder Waddock described it as the Shots' best half of the season: "At times we've played some really good football since Martin Kuhl and I have been in charge but that has to be the best 45 minutes we've played since I've been here."

Stevenage should have taken an early lead, but Mitchell Cole dragged his shot wide after an uncharacteristic error by Winfield. But that was as good as it got for the visitors, as the Shots took over. There have been some notable attacking first half displays this season at the Rec, especially against Grays Athletic and Woking, but on this occasion the Shots reached another level.

Aside from the three goals, Winfield had a header saved from a Chalmers long-throw, Hudson twice fired just wide, Hylton rolled another shot just past the post and Stevenage keeper Alan Julian made a magnificent save from Harding's barn-storming free kick, after a fine run from Straker.

Joel Grant celebrates his opening goal with Danny Hylton.

The first and third goals were sublime. In the ninth minute Hudson had a shot blocked and Gier's clever pass freed Chalmers, whose lofted ball into the area was swept past Julian by Joel Grant.

For the third, on the half hour, Grant's silky skills bamboozled the Stevenage defence yet again, before Hudson took over, dragging the ball into space with a clever flick and crossing for Hylton to touch home. In between, John Grant was tripped in the area and picked himself up to score from the spot.

Inevitably, the Shots struggled to rediscover their amazing verve after the break but while lively susbstitute Gavin Grant did head a goal back for Borough on 62 minutes, the Shots avoided the nail-biting finishes in the aforementioned Grays and Woking matches, and effectively killed the game.

Not a lot happened in the last half an hour and Harding, keeping possession with assurance in the middle, and Day and Winfield, with a series of meaty, well-timed tackles, must take much of the credit. Nikki Bull, on a rare moment of activity, also made a good catch under pressure.

But it was Day, restored to the team in Charles' absence, who deserved particular praise, after torrid displays not so long ago in defeats to Forest Green Rovers and York City. "I'm delighted for Rhys," said Waddock afterwards. "He was outstanding tonight, as was Dave Winfield."

> **❝** *We have players in the squad who know that if given an opportunity they must take it and the great thing is that players are coming in and doing that.* **❞**

The manager was relaxed enough to join in with the East Bank's chant of "C'mon the Shots, C'mon the Shots" towards the end, even bobbing to the beat. Or perhaps he and his side just like to play up to the camera. After all, Aldershot have a perfect record of played three, won three, live on Setanta this season, which bodes well for their next live match, the key trip to Torquay's Plainmoor in two weeks' time.

Joel Grant leads Stevenage on a merry dance.

DAYS THINKS IT ALL OVER

19 February 2008

I've just watched Sunday's match on television. I knew we'd played well but seeing that first half, with the benefit of all the replays, some of our play was unbelievable.

It was a great performance from the lads. The team spirit has been good all season but the dressing room was absolutely buzzing after the final whistle. We were all ecstatic. The Gaffer was getting quite enthusiastic too. Of course we know that we must now make sure we push on from the win, but by beating one of the league's fancied teams, live on television, I think we've put out a bit of a statement to the rest of the league. I don't think anyone was too surprised that we didn't reach the same heights in the second half. The Gaffer said to us at half-time: "You've been absolutely fantastic but don't you dare take your foot off the pedal." He made it clear that we'd be in for a right rollicking if we didn't keep going and, while they scored a goal, I think we did ensure that we followed his other main instruction well: if they do get a goal back, then stay calm and don't panic.

We had a good crowd, despite it being on television and on a Sunday evening. The fans have been brilliant all season but I think in the last two home games, against Cambridge and Stevenage, that we're beginning to see the numbers go up a little as we head towards crunch time in the season. It's great to see.

Anthony Charles' suspension meant that I was recalled to the team by the Gaffer. It was great to be back in the side for such a big game, live on television too, and to be back captaining from on the pitch. I think that was probably the best I've played this season. I was very happy with the way Dave Winfield and I played at the back. I've been disappointed not to be in the team for league matches of late but the team has done well without me, so I couldn't complain.

Besides, I think only if your team was in mid-table, with nothing to play for, can you really ever want the person

in front of you in the team selection to do badly. But that's not what I'm about anyway. Watching from the bench, I've been willing Dave to do well because that means the team will do well, which is what we all want. Charlesy said to me and Dave after the Stevenage game: "Well, after that display from you two, it looks like it's going to be my turn to be the benchwarmer," and Dave and I nodded and said, "Too right, mate."

But we'll have to see. Dave and I feel we put in a good performance but that's no guarantee that the Gaffer will pick us in the next game. It's the way it should be; competition for places is good for us all.

Some people were suggesting that I should shave my hair short again, like it was early in the season, as that might help me rediscover my form. Well, I've cut my hair and I played well, but the truth is a bit different…

I was planning to grow my hair long and develop a bit of a mullet, just for a laugh and a throwback to old fashions! I got as far as actually having it cut at the sides so that the mullet was there, but it just didn't work. The only option was to shave my whole head as quickly as possible!

After the Hampshire Cup tie against Basingstoke we turn to the FA Trophy against Tamworth. We're still in a number of competitions and want to win every game. The Gaffer makes sure we concentrate on one game at a time, but of course we are all aware that if we beat Tamworth then we are just a two-legged semi-final away from playing at Wembley. None of us can dismiss that totally from our minds, but first we must make sure that we get past Tamworth, which won't be easy.

The league game away at Torquay is fast approaching too, and we have Kidderminster to play in the league before then. But we have the cups to concentrate on first, so we must forget about the league for now.

ALDERSHOT TOWN 1
(Phillips 47)

BASINGSTOKE TOWN 2
(Warner 85, Fitzgerald 109)

19 February 2008
Hampshire Senior Cup

LINE-UP

Jaimez-Ruiz, Sackey, Milletti, Koo-Boothe, Newman (Hardy 60), Davies, Soares, Donnelly, Elvins, Simmonds (Huggins 44), Phillips (Scott 77).

The dream of the quadruple perished in the freezing fog at the Recreation Ground on Tuesday evening. In truth, however, even the Setanta Shield ranks above the Hampshire Cup in Aldershot's quest for glory this season, so Basingstoke Town's 2-1 win, clinched deep into extra time, was hardly the end of the world.

In the Blue Square Premier and, to a lesser extent, the FA Trophy, Gary Waddock's team have far bigger fish to fry. The league is a great white shark; the Hampshire Cup is a mere whitebait. But Waddock was still disappointed to lose, given that Aldershot were the holders and that his side missed a host of clear-cut chances and led 1-0 for most of the second half of normal time.

Louie Soares, who started alongside a scattering of other first-team squad regulars – Scott Davies, Rob Elvins and Ricky Newman – was most profligate, seeing a first-half penalty saved onto the post by Basingstoke keeper Chris Tardiff and missing from four one-on-one duels with Tardiff. Soares, who played the second half up front, showed he can time a run superbly, but his finishing was woeful.

"Soaresy could have gone away with two match balls," said Waddock afterwards. "He's quite upset with himself but there's no need to be. He's done really well for us this season." Besides, if Soares is saving a goal or two for the league or the Trophy, then no Shots fans will be complaining.

In fairness to Soares, it was from his fierce shot that

Lewis Phillips tucked home a rebound to give Aldershot a 47th minute lead on his first-team debut.

"Lewis was a bit tense and nervous," said Waddock.

"But games like this are a good experience for young lads. We asked Lewis at half time to get in the box more from wide left and he responded and took his chance well."

Warner's pace aside, Basingstoke, who fielded a full-strength side, threatened little in the first half. One of their brighter moments came when referee Rob Styles – yes, the Premiership official – inadvertently set up a Basingstoke attack, but it came to nothing and Styles' blushes were spared.

Styles was short of back-up and Aldershot first team coach Martin Kuhl even had to carry out fourth official duties whenever Aldershot made a substitution; a case of poacher turned gamekeeper, but Kuhl appeared to see the funny side.

Waddock, however, was less jovial after the match. "We had enough chances to win comfortably but didn't take them and therefore didn't deserve to win," he said. "As a result we are out of the cup."

The manager agreed that the withdrawal of Ricky Newman on the hour was key. Newman, forced off to protect a knee injury, had marshalled the Aldershot defence superbly and George Hardy, his replacement, and Nathan Koo-Boothe, never looked comfortable.

The biggest cheer of the night came in the 77th minute,

Gary Waddock had some harsh words after the Shots lost out on the Hampshire Cup.

when Ryan Scott made his first appearance since breaking his leg at the end of last season. Although he looked understandably off the pace and a little hesitant, he will have benefited hugely from what became a 45-minute cameo.

"I was delighted for Ryan," said Waddock. "It's a big plus to have him back."

But Basingstoke looked the more cohesive side – unsurprisingly – the longer the game went on. Warner's neatly-taken 85th minute equaliser came as no surprise, given that he had rattled the inside of the post three minutes earlier and Basingstoke had spurned a number of late chances and forced two good saves from Mikhael Jaimez-Ruiz.

The Shots did rally in extra time. Soares' most glaring miss came in the 99th minute, after good work by Scott Donnelly and substitute Danny Huggins, and Davies

also enjoyed a superb run along the goalline, but no Aldershot player could make his cutback.

> **"***If you don't take your chances then you don't win games.***"**
>
> Gary Waddock

But the last word belonged to former Brentford striker Scott Fitzgerald. It wasn't exactly a classic to rival The Great Gatsby, but his diving header in the 108th minute closed Aldershot's Hampshire Cup chapter for 2008. But the good news is that there are still plenty of chances for the story of Aldershot's season to have a happy ending.

TAMWORTH 1

(Williams 82)

ALDERSHOT TOWN 2

(Winfield 81, Hudson 90)

23 February 2008
FA Trophy quarter-final

LINE-UP

Bull, Gier, Straker, Day, Winfield, Chalmers, Hudson, Harding (Davies 55), John Grant (Elvins 44), Hylton (Soares 62), Joel Grant.

Aldershot have earned plenty of plaudits for their up-tempo, free-flowing football this season, but on Saturday it was all about strength, stamina and character as they edged out a determined Tamworth side to reach the FA Carlsberg Trophy semi-finals.

The game began with Tamworth determined to assert themselves. They had a couple of chances in the opening 25 minutes, with Rhys Day blocking a rasping shot from former Nottingham Forest star Des Lyttle, and Nikki Bull reacting smartly to keep out a ball that deflected off Ben Harding from a Jonty Richter cross.

But it was Aldershot who went closest to posting the initial score just before the 30-minute mark. Joel Grant's quick-footed trickery outwitted defender Craig McAughtrie, whose challenge merely succeeded in toppling the skilful winger just outside the left-hand side of the penalty area.

Up stepped Harding to mastermind the free kick and his rasping left-footed shot forced keeper Alex Cisak to tip the ball onto the crossbar. As space in the middle of the park became tighter as the half moved on, so a little more 'niggle' entered proceedings. That manifested itself in a couple of cases of 'handbags', most notably between Gier and the 'in-your-face' Chris Nurse, who squared up on the halfway line. Both were shown a yellow card.

Shots fans shared a collective sharp intake of breath as John Grant was taken off on a stretcher with his left leg in a brace after 44 minutes, having been injured by a crude challenge from Tamworth captain Adie Smith, for which the defender was booked. Fortunately, Gary Waddock later confirmed that there is hope that Grant will appear again this season.

The second half began with Tamworth on the attack and, after 47 minutes, they carved out a real opportunity. Sheldon worked well done the flank and his cross found Nurse, whose fierce header cannoned off the bar.

Despite the endeavours of both teams, attempts on goal were at a premium. An exception was when Jamie Reed missed out in a one-on-one with Bull, lobbing the ball over the bar on 71 minutes. Ten minutes later, though, a mini goal-fest was triggered when Aldershot won a corner. Davies took the kick and his excellent delivery was met by the head of the soaring Winfield, who planted the ball in the back of the net from six yards.

That sense of relief and joy lasted all of 30 seconds as Tamworth went straight down the other end and equalised after a defensive mix-up between Bull and Anthony Straker, which allowed Jake Sheridan to shoot into an empty net.

Unbelievably, after the 70 minutes of stalemate, both sides had chances to win the game during added time – a Winfield volley went just over the bar, while Tamworth's Williams had only Bull to beat when shooting wide. From the goal kick, the long ball forward found its way to Hudson who was out on the right-hand side of the penalty area. From 20 yards he used his left foot to curl the ball over the many bodies in the area, over Cisak and into the far corner of the goal.

Whether it was a deliberate shot of an intended cross, the result was mass celebration from everyone red and blue, and despair for the hard-working home team. Shots' manager Waddock said: "Tamworth were excellent and for long periods we were second best. Kirk's goal was a 'get-out-of-jail' card really and we were very fortunate."

" We've learned a lot from this game and we still have lots to work on, but we need to show that we can stand up to battles such as this. "

Gary Waddock

HARDING AND CHALMERS FOR ENGLAND

There was further evidence of Aldershot Town's outstanding season last week, when dynamic midfield duo Ben Harding and Lewis Chalmers swapped the red of Aldershot for the white of England.

© Phil Mingo / Pinnacle

Manager Paul Fairclough had plenty of young non-league midfielders to choose from but it was little surprise that he picked the Aldershot pair for the England C international against Wales U23s at Exeter City's St James Park ground.

The two are arguably the best central midfield axis in non-league football, with Chalmers' northern bite complemented superbly by Harding's southern swagger.

The two helped England to a 2-1 win in Group A of the International Challenge Trophy.

Chalmers is an England C regular, after Fairclough first called him up when he was still an Altrincham player last season, but Wednesday was a debut for Harding. Not that

England representation was new to Harding, having played for his country as a junior. "I played for England at U15, U16 and U17 level, alongside current full internationals like David Bentley and Glen Johnson," said Harding.

"I'm a pretty patriotic guy and it's an absolute honour to represent my country. I was a bit surprised to get the call up but I do think I have been putting some good performances in for Aldershot."

Chalmers certainly enjoys having Harding alongside him: "I'm always very pleased to get called up by England but this week was especially good, with Ben in there with me," he said.

"The pitch wasn't the

best and we had to play a longer-ball game than at Aldershot, but it was great all the same. Ben and I complement each other. We know where to be on the pitch in relation to the other. Ben is technically very good and makes things happen, while I am a bit better defensively, I think," said Chalmers.

Harding agreed: "Lewis is superb at breaking the opposition play up and quickly giving me the ball."

Waddock and Shots coach Martin Kuhl are both former professional midfielders and Harding and Chalmers are benefiting from their tuition.

"I think Gary and Martin have helped my game massively since I arrived from Altrincham," said Chalmers. "My decision-

making has improved hugely. I understand better that doing the simple thing can sometimes be best."

Harding agreed: "As ex-midfield players they pass on tips and help us all out. Martin Kuhl is fantastic in training."

If Harding and Chalmers stay fit and available and continue playing as they have, then maybe they, like Waddock and Kuhl, will soon ply their trade in the Football League.

Harding has been there before, with MK Dons, and sees no reason why Aldershot cannot win promotion. He said: "We know there is a long way to go but we are sure that we are good enough to do it. The team spirit here is so good."

CRAWLEY TOWN 2

(Pittman 54, 89)

ALDERSHOT TOWN 6

(Day 59, 117, Hudson 63, Hylton 93, Joel Grant 94, Donnelly 101)

26 February 2008
Setanta Shield quarter-final

LINE-UP

Jaimez-Ruiz, Smith, Milletti, Winfield (Day 45), Charles, Davies, Soares (Chalmers 101), Donnelly, Elvins, Hylton, Hudson (Joel Grant 71).

The importance of the Setanta Shield to Aldershot Town was reflected in Gary Waddock's absence from the Broadfield Stadium on Tuesday evening.

Promotion to the Football League is Aldershot's priority and Waddock chose to watch Torquay United, the Shots' rival for the one automatic promotion spot, leaving Martin Kuhl in charge of the match at Crawley.

But his players still performed magnificently with a scintillating display of pacy, attacking football, that was finally rewarded in extra time, with four goals that made a mockery of the 2-2 stalemate over 90 minutes.

> " We are in another semi-final, which is fantastic news for the club. "
>
> Gary Waddock

Scott Donnelly, who put in another dynamic performance in midfield, claimed the pick of the goals, running on to Lewis Chalmers' wonderful pass and outrageously chipping home in the 102nd minute, making the score 5-2 and putting the gloss on a sublime first period of extra time, in which the Shots scored three times.

Danny Hylton, who rounded Crawley keeper Ashey Bayes with consummate ease and Joel Grant, who excelled as a substitute against Crawley's tiring defenders, also found the net in that period.

Rhys Day added the sixth goal three minutes from time with a looping header from Scott Davies' free kick. That goal was a pretty mundane finish as far as Day was concerned, compared to an earlier 59th minute thunderbolt which had made the score 1-1, five minutes after Jon Paul Pittman had headed Crawley ahead.

Day controlled Donnelly's free kick, swivelled and thumped a right-footed half-volley into the top corner. Much more finishing like that from Day and Waddock can call off his search for a new striker, should John Grant's recovery from injury take longer than is hoped.

Four minutes later Aldershot had turned the game on its head. Hudson, set up by good play by Louie Soares and Rob Elvins, raced clear and confidently slipped the ball under Bayes for his tenth goal of the season, which have all come since mid-December. But Crawley enjoyed plenty of good moments in normal time and Jaimez-Ruiz made a string of fine saves to keep them out, the pick of them touching a Dannie Bulman shot onto the post, with Mustapha Carayol missing woefully from the rebound.

Crawley hit the bar ten minutes later, through substitute Magno Vieira. So, perhaps it was deserved when, in the 86th minute, Pittman turned in the equaliser after substitute Ollie Allen, son of Clive, had outsmarted Day and crossed from the by-line.

Crawley celebrated wildly but if manager Steve Evans thought Aldershot would lie down at the prospect of extra time, he was sorely mistaken. Crawley's defence had been stretched all night by Aldershot's pace and movement and now the Shots found their finishing touch.

> " In the end we had a bit more quality to our finishing. We have fantastic ability in the squad "
>
> Martin Kuhl

DAYS THINKS IT ALL OVER

28 February 2008

It's great news about Junior Mendes signing. I know him from our days together at Mansfield Town [Day and Mendes were in the Mansfield team that lost the 2004 Division Three play-off final to Huddersfield Town] and I spoke to him a month or so ago and asked him whether he was free to come and train with us. He's a good pro, he's fit and I can see him nicking a few goals. What's more, he will work his nuts off – it's a big plus to have him.

I wasn't even sure he was in the country as I knew he'd had a bit of bad luck at Notts County and didn't really get along with the management there, and then he had a setback with an injury while trying to get with a club in Armenia.

He's a good striker but I thought I had better show him the way the things are done, hence the two goals in the Setanta Shield match at Crawley on Tuesday. I don't think I've ever scored a better goal with my foot than that right-footed half-volley, but maybe I've preferred one or two headed goals in my career, being a defender. To be honest, I'm often the top scorer in training, so it's not that unusual, and I let the lads know about it. Actually, I set myself a target of ten goals this season and I'm half way there, with taking a few penalties too.

We needed my goal on Tuesday but that was just typical of the way we've played this season. We've gone behind but we seem to have the ability to up the tempo and have a good few more gears to go into, like for Kirk Hudson's goal and then the goals in extra time.

I'm pretty pleased with my form right now. There's no hiding from the fact that I had a two-game dip in form last month [in the league defeats to Forest Green Rovers and York City]. I still can't really explain it – I prepared just the same, eating the same as usual, didn't have a drink and was resting well – but I guess no player can go through a season and perform to the very best of their ability in every game.

Then Charlesey was suspended and I got back in. The gaffer has said all along that if you are given the shirt and perform well, then you will keep it, and he's been true to his word.

I think in the last few weeks we've seen the squad expand from about 16 or 17 players to nearer 20, any of which could come into a first-team match and do a job. Players like Scott Donnelly and now Junior. Some squads have three or four weaker players but I don't think we do. It keeps us all on our toes and is a brilliant situation for the manager.

Of course there's Ryan Williams too, who might possibly come into the picture. I was on the internet with him earlier in the week while he was choosing a pair of new boots, so, he must have a return to training in mind. They are a fancy Nike pair, a bit too colourful for my liking, with black, grey and red, and his name on the side. He's pretty upbeat and if he can come back into the picture for the last few games it will be great for him and the club.

The FA Trophy and the thought of playing at Wembley is enough to keep us all buzzing and happy at the moment, without even thinking of the league. Talking of the league, as far as I can see we have 14 cup finals ahead of us and we need to win as many of them as possible.

Kidderminster will be tough on Saturday and then, of course, we have Torquay on Monday night. Our preparation for the fixture will be very professional. After playing on Saturday afternoon, we'll be in on Sunday morning for a warm-down from the day before and then we travel down to Devon on Sunday for an overnight stay in a hotel. Then we'll train down there on Monday morning ahead of the game – and hopefully the right result.

JUNIOR MENDES JOINS

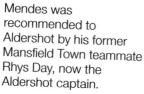

New Shots striker Junior Mendes said he is 'very excited' to be joining the Shots, after signing for the club on Thursday.

Mendes was recommended to Aldershot by his former Mansfield Town teammate Rhys Day, now the Aldershot captain.

"I've been training with Aldershot for a few weeks after Rhys recommended me to the club," said Mendes, speaking as news broke of his signing. "At first I wasn't sure what would come from training with the lads, I was just happy to keep fit."

Mendes has had a frustrating season to date, leaving Notts County after just a few games and then getting injured while training with a club in Armenia.

"But things have worked out really well," said Mendes. "From the start I got along with the boys, the manager and the coaches. I felt relaxed from the off and everyone has been very welcoming. Attitudes like that are priceless in football."

Mendes has yet to watch his new teammates in a match, but has seen enough in training to impress him.

"I can see why they are top of the league, that's for sure," he said. "Obviously I know Rhys well and I recognise a few faces from having played against them in the Football League before.

"Everything about the club has impressed me. It is like a Football League club, the way it is run and the training techniques.

"I'm not sure I can say I am match fit, but I am definitely fit. While I need to wean myself back into playing matches, hopefully it will not be too slow a process. All the boys are buzzing, with the promotion bid and the FA Trophy run."

Mendes, 31, scored 21 goals in 120 appearances for St Mirren after being released by Chelsea in the mid-90s and has since played for, among others, Mansfield and Huddersfield Town.

He has made two international appearances for the Caribbean island of Montserrat, scoring one goal.

"I've been interested in a few forwards," said Shots manager Waddock on Thursday afternoon. "Rhys recommended Junior to me and he's been with us for two to three weeks."

The Shots had to wait to get international clearance for Mendes, but Waddock was also keen to have a good look at the player.

"He knows the way we play and our style and know we need to get him into games," said Waddock. "He's scored goals in both England and Scotland and looks fit and sharp. He's a livewire, nippy type of forward and athletic too. He's the type of player I like and will be in the squad for the Kidderminster game on Saturday.

"We have quite a young group here and he brings plenty of experience with him too," added Waddock

Mendes agreed: "I think the most successful football sides have a nice blend of youth and experience and I can help provide some experience and hopefully goals too," said Mendes.

"I am raring to go."

ALDERSHOT TOWN 2
(Hylton 5, Harding 66)

KIDDERMINSTER HARRIERS 1
(Barnes-Homer 3)

LINE-UP

Line-up Bull, Gier (Soares 55), Day, Charles, Straker, Joel Grant, Chalmers, Harding, Hudson (Davies 55). Elvins (Mendes 55), Hylton.

"Kidderminster are a good team. We can't afford to be caught short and we won't be."

Gary Waddock

Victories in football come in different styles and Aldershot Town needed patience and tenacity to snare all three points against Kidderminster Harriers on Saturday.

There were mixed emotions from an early stage. First came news that Torquay United had slumped to defeat in the day's early kick-off at Grays Athletic. Then the Shots found themselves a goal down after just three minutes – and one that was down to defensive error rather than attacking guile.

Chris McKenzie in the visiting goal launched a long kick towards the East Bank and Anthony Charles slipped, allowing Matthew Barnes-Homes to nip in and lift the ball over the advancing keeper from just inside the left-hand side of the penalty area.

That goal might have deflated the confidence of many teams, and it certainly left the home fans in a momentary spasm of silent reflection, but within two minutes the Shots were back on level terms and the fans were singing again.

The hard-working Lewis Chalmers received the ball in the middle of the Kidderminster half, and cleverly made some room for himself to dink a ball into area. Charles, who was looking for redemption, managed to get his head to the ball eight yards out but keeper McKenzie reacted well to palm the ball away to his right. Unfortunately for him, young striker Danny Hylton was on hand to poke the ball home from inside the six-yard box, despite the presence of two Kidderminster defenders.

Kidderminster had their moments, too, with the lively Brian Smikle often a provider down the right flank. On 11 minutes he got to the goal line and his cross spelled all sorts of trouble as it fizzed across the goalmouth but Rob Gier anticipated better than the forwards to clear the ball in his usual efficient fashion.

Just a minute later it was the turn of Luke Jones to break free on left and his early cross was inches away from the head of Russell Penn, who charged in late on the far post.

On 24 minutes Charles played a low free kick into the area and Grant, on the edge of the box, redirected the ball wide right to Gier. His cross was headed goalwards by Charles from eight yards but keeper McKenzie had no trouble gathering the ball.

Danny Hylton (second from left) has just put the Shots level.

Ben Harding hails his winner.

surprise when, on 66 minutes, Aldershot took the lead with yet another Harding special. This time it was from 20 yards, using the outside of his right boot, and the ball was always edging wide of the keeper and inside the right-hand post.

Never more vulnerable than after scoring, the Shots had a scare from kick-off. Kidderminster broke down the left and a good ball in from Paul Bignot went across the home side's six-yard box but the incoming Smikle was just unable to lay a boot on the ball. That seemed to spur the visitors and on 68 minutes the introduction of striker Iyseden Christie saw them switch to 4-4-2.

There was nearly a sting in the tail for the Shots, two minutes into the three of added time. The muscular Christie, played in by Russell Penn, found himself one-on-one with Bull but the home keeper spread himself and stopped Christie's shot with his legs, saving a vital three points.

That was a point echoed by Waddock, who said: "Nikki won it for us with that save. He had not had anything to do all second-half but his concentration was superb."

The manager was also full of praise for Hylton:

> *" He does not stop. He just gives 100% and that is what he is all about. "*

Chalmers worked hard to set up plenty of chances.

With just over eight minutes to go until half time, Kidderminster's dangerman Smikle again created trouble down the right but when his pass picked out Michael McGrath 18 yards from goal, the resulting shot went unerringly into the arms of Bull. The Shots broke to the other end but Ben Harding was brought down by a crude challenge 20 yards out.

After the break, Chalmers won the ball inside the Harriers' half before despatching it to Joel Grant on the left of area. Grant cut inside with the sole intention of getting a shot away. He succeeded in doing that but without accuracy and the ball flew over the bar.

By now manager Gary Waddock had obviously decided he needed to change things around a bit, so he turned to the Jose Mourinho manual and made a triple substitution on 55 minutes. Elvins, Gier and a subdued Kirk Hudson made way for Louie Soares, Scott Davies and new striker Junior Mendes, so there was no mistaking that attack was the word on Waddock's mind.

The impact was there for all to see, and with the momentum from the home side building, it was no

3 March 2008

TORQUAY UNITED 1
(Phillips 63)

ALDERSHOT TOWN 2
(Hylton 6, Davies 90)

The Promised Land is in sight for the Shots. Perhaps it's not one of milk and honey, but the fish of Grimsby and cockles of Morecambe will taste just as sweet to Aldershot fans, if they do play there in the Football League next season.

But there were cockles in Torquay too on Monday – the cockles of Aldershot hearts, warmed by Scott Davies' dramatic injury time winner, on a wintry evening on the English Riviera.

Some might suggest that it's a matter of 'when' not 'if' the Shots are promoted, now that Aldershot have opened up an 11-point lead over Torquay United, thanks to Monday night's 2-1 win. But Aldershot still have 12 games to play and Torquay have a game in hand, so Gary Waddock and his players will remain cautious.

On the night, it wasn't plain sailing at Plainmoor. Torquay were unlucky to lose and, in a tale of two keepers, the Shots were indebted to a string of excellent saves from Nikki Bull, especially in the second half, and Waddock paid tribute to his performance:

> " *The strikers and other outfield players get the plaudits, but it's just amazing how many points and games Nikki has already won for us over the season already.* "

Aldershot, on the other hand, took full advantage of poor keeping from Torquay's young custodian Mikkel Andersen who, like Davies, is on loan from Reading, but endured a miserable evening in comparison to Aldershot's flame-haired Irishman.

But that is Aldershot all over: they know how to win tight games, as their Blue Square Premier record of

Danny Hylton gives Aldershot the early lead.

© Herald Express, Torquay

25 victories from 34 games illustrates. On Monday they stood firm under Torquay's second half pressure. Bull was outstanding but, after a shaky start, Anthony Charles was especially obdurate at left-back, fully justifying Waddock's decision to go for his height and experience ahead of Anthony Straker.

The Gulls, on the other hand, were chasing the game after Danny Hylton made them pay for a mistake as early as the sixth minute. Andersen came to claim Ben Harding's long ball but he and Mark Ellis hesitated and Hylton impishly darted between them and headed goalwards, nonchalantly rolling the ball into the empty net.

Although Kaid Mohamed wasted two good first half chances for Torquay – Bull making an excellent save at his near post for one of them – Aldershot looked the more assured side.

Joel Grant was the best attacking player on the pitch before the break and gave stand-in right-back Lee

Gary Waddock was delighted after the victory.

Mansell a torrid time. After a nervous start Rhys Day and Dave Winfield grew in stature and Rob Gier got to grips with Torquay's flying winger, Chris Zebroski.

In the middle, Harding and Lewis Chalmers had quiet games by their high standards but, with Davies tucking in and bolstering the midfield, Aldershot had a solid formation. Certainly, while it was a surprise that Waddock left Kirk Hudson on the bench, Davies' energetic display fully justified his inclusion, even before his goal.

Torquay, desperate for the three points, inevitably came hard at the Shots after the break. Day blocked a Phillips shot and then Bull denied the same player, this time after a mis-kick from Day. Ten minutes later, in the 63rd minute, Torquay were level. Substitute Danny Stevens made space for Mansell to cross and Phillips' header flashed past Bull.

Hudson and Junior Mendes added pace and energy up front late on, but, at 1-1, Aldershot appeared fairly happy with their lot, especially after Chalmers fell awkwardly in the 85th minute and the game was held up for five minutes before he could be stretchered off.

But Aldershot have the ability and belief to make good news from bad: in the fourth minute of injury time, Mendes chased down a long ball from Charles and inadvertently fed Davies. He controlled the ball and thumped a left-footed volley across Andersen. The keeper should probably have saved the shot. But no one from Aldershot cared, as the 1000-strong fans – and even Waddock – danced with delight as the ball nestled in the far corner of the net.

“ *The fans were absolutely brilliant. They definitely contributed to our win and we really can't thank them enough.* **”**

Gary Waddock

Aldershot are not there yet and tricky fixtures lie ahead, but the smell of the Promised Land is in the air – and it's as real as the salty sea breeze of Torquay.

DAYS THINKS IT ALL OVER

6 March 2008

The squad is still buzzing after Monday's win at Torquay. But at training on Thursday Martin Kuhl really got into us. He doesn't mince his words. He reminded us in no uncertain terms that we haven't won anything yet.

We know that and our feet are very much on the ground. But at least, now it's been and gone, we can talk about Torquay. Winning like that certainly made the journey home a pretty easy one - and for the fantastic fans who made the long trip too, no doubt.

It was just brilliant to win like that, with virtually the last kick, after we had been under the cosh a bit in the second half. From the back, I saw the ball bouncing up and I said to myself 'go on, Scotty, hit it' – and he did. To be honest, great strike that it was, I think the keeper should have saved it, but we certainly don't care about that.

We had our usual huddle after the game. Everyone can contribute, but it's normally led by me, as captain, or by Bully (Nikki Bull), as a senior player. Bully was pretty emotional after the win, but the victory meant a lot to everyone. Bully's been at the club a while and knows it and the fans so well. He played superbly too, and that always adds to the emotion.

To be honest, I simply can't believe that Bully is still playing football in the Conference, rather than the Football League. At the back, we are so fortunate to play in the knowledge that he's behind us to help out, if we make a mistake, or the opposition break through. If Bully's confronted with a one-on-one, there's a great chance that he will make a save, which has been so important to us this season.

He's a really good guy, too. If any of the young lads have a problem or need advice, or just need a chat, then they go to Bully. He's simply a top man.

I hadn't heard that Paul Parker, the Setanta summariser, often refers to me as Rhys Davies, rather than Rhys Day. Oh well. But I'm simply not having him saying Richard

Gere, rather than Rob Gier...I think it's fair to say that Richard Gere has just a little bit more about him than Giero! As for Paul Parker, maybe we'll just have to start calling him Peter Parker (Spider Man)!

Now we turn to the FA Trophy semi-final first leg at Ebbsfleet on Saturday. It is good to go into the game knowing that we got the right result at Torquay and now have a nice lead in the league. That was our aim and we've done it.

But we still have so many games to come and while we are eager to get to Wembley, we have to get past Ebbsfleet. There's Histon in the league next week too, and then around Easter we have a huge number of games, now also including Droylsden on the Thursday afterwards.

The Gaffer made changes for the Torquay game and he said to us last week that there will be changes in the games to come. He and Kuhly will pick a team that is right at the time the game is played and for the opposition we face. To be honest, as a player, so long as we keep on winning, then it's no bother. We simply need to keep on getting the right results.

Junior Mendes is settling in well and he played for the reserves on Wednesday and scored in the 1-1 draw at Leyton Orient. He is now another one pushing for a starting place.

I'm quite pleased with the early kick-off at Ebbsfleet because it means I should be able to watch the latter stages of Wales' huge rugby match in Ireland. It's a massive game for the boys and the nation, as we chase the Triple Crown and Grand Slam. They have done brilliantly, beating the likes of England, as I enjoy pointing out.

I know Lee Byrne, the fullback, and Shane Williams well and speak to them quite often. Hopefully both Aldershot and Wales can go and get a good win on Saturday.

EBBSFLEET UNITED 3

(McPhee 6 pen, 37 pen, McCarthy 78)

ALDERSHOT TOWN 1

(Mendes 76)

8 March 2008
FA Trophy semi-final
first leg

Gary Waddock is always at pains to protect his players. Public criticism from the manager of his Aldershot squad is rarer than the Shots drawing a game this season – and that's only happened three times.

Sixteen wins from their last 18 home matches, mean that the road to the final at Wembley in May is far from closed. But how Aldershot could have done with a draw on Saturday in the FA Trophy semi-final first leg, in which they crashed to a 3-1 defeat away to Ebbsfleet United, on a blustery day on the banks of the Thames estuary.

Waddock, typically, did not single out individuals for a public dressing down, but perhaps that was more because there was no need to: aside from keeper Bull, Waddock felt that all the other ten players had let him and coach Martin Kuhl down.

"The way I felt at half-time, I'd have liked to have changed the lot and brought on ten new players," said Waddock. "All season we have worked hard and closed teams down, but I saw nothing of that in the first half."

Aldershot's midfield tenacity of old was sadly lacking from the side's play. Ben Harding had his quietest game for a long while and clearly missed his usual midfield sidekick, Lewis Chalmers, out with ankle ligament trouble.

To be fair, Scott Davies, who moved inside to fill Chalmers' role, worked tirelessly throughout, but he and Harding could not gain control of the game. Nor could Rob Elvins and Danny Hylton get any change out of Ebbsfleet's experienced centre backs, Paul McCarthy and Peter Hawkins. It was two tyros against two titans; or, for a match played adjacent to the north Kent marshes, two Pips against two Magwitches.

Aldershot's season still has great expectations but they had little answer to Ebbsfleet's great big front two of John Akinde and Chukki Eribenne, who, feeding off balls over the top, were too quick and strong for Anthony Charles and Dave Winfield, who was preferred to club captain Rhys Day.

The two penalties were all too similar. First, after six minutes, Winfield hacked down Eribenne, who had got goal side of the Aldershot defender. Perhaps the foul was outside the area; but perhaps Winfield should have been sent off as the last defender, rather than just booked. In the 37th minute it was Charles caught napping by a ball over the top. Perhaps Akinde went down very easily after minimal contact; but perhaps Charles was lucky to stay on the pitch. His yellow card, his tenth of the season, is due to rule him out of the second leg.

In between the penalties – Chris McPhee gave Bull no chance with either – Stacy Long, who gave Rob Gier the run around all afternoon, went close and Bull and his defence survived an almighty melee.

Waddock took the maximum option available to him and made three changes at the break, bringing on Junior Mendes, Kirk Hudson and Day for Hylton, Joel Grant and Winfield. The changes made a significant difference and, in a hugely entertaining second half, 1-1 was probably a fair reflection, with Mendes pulling a goal back with 16 minutes to go – his first for the club – before more defensive lapses allowed Ebbsfleet captain McCarthy immediately to restore his side's two-goal advantage.

In the dying minutes both sides should have scored. Akinde dragged a shot wide when clear through, before Hudson selfishly shot from a narrow angle, when a cross would have provided Elvins with a tap-in. Crucially, Bull saved at the feet of Long in injury time.

> **" All credit to Ebbsfleet, but ultimately that first half has cost us this afternoon's game. "**
>
> Gary Waddock

11 March 2008

ALDERSHOT TOWN 3
(Davies 12, Hudson 32, 65)

HISTON 1
(Murray 63)

A workman-like performance enabled Aldershot Town to pick up an important three points against Histon on Tuesday night, the perfect response to the Shots' disappointing display at Ebbsfleet United last Saturday.

The victory was given added value by the defeat of Torquay United at Halifax Town, which leaves Aldershot 13 points clear of second-placed Cambridge United, with both teams having 11 league fixtures remaining.

The opening exchanges were a scrappy affair, although Histon did threaten on six minutes when the lively Jack Midson fired over. However, it was Aldershot that opened the scoring on 12 minutes. Scott Davies was the beneficiary when the ball broke loose midway in the Histon half, and the young midfielder was quick to register that he was within shooting range, despatching a 22-yard scorcher to put the Shots ahead.

Shots' followers had their hearts in their mouths from the restart – a time when Aldershot have been vulnerable on occasions this season – as the ball found its way to Danny Wright in the penalty area. Only two timely interventions by Anthony Charles and smart keeping by Nikki Bull prevented an equaliser.

The near lapse prompted assistant manager Martin Kuhl, angry at the loss of concentration, to bellow: "When we score, get back on the game."

The game had plenty of hustle and bustle in the middle of the pitch, but little opportunity for the home side to get the ball down, as Histon executed their game plan of denying the Shots time and space with good effect.

Goalmouth action was hardly at a premium, and both sides tried their luck from long range with Histon's Adrian Cambridge shooting over the bar. Aldershot's Anthony Straker finished off a trademark charge down the left-side of centre with a 35-yard swerving and dipping shot that visiting keeper Danny Naisbitt tipped wide.

Scott Davies jumps for joy after his early goal.

The home side gradually began to dictate possession with Charles and Davies coming close on the half hour, but a second goal was needed to ease the fans' nerves. Fortunately, it was not long in coming, and it was fitting that Kirk Hudson should be the man to score the goal, finishing with aplomb from 10 yards after an expertly executed assist from the lively Straker.

Kirk Hudson lauds the first of his two goals.

Histon managed their first shot on target after 40 minutes when Antonio Murray showed good pace to give himself an opportunity, but was no match for Bull, who pulled off a smart reaction save to put the ball out for a corner.

Hudson has had quite a time of late, voted Blue Square Premier player of the month for February and on Monday signing a new two-year contract.

" I am delighted that Kirk has committed himself to the club for the next two seasons. He has the ability to push his career on and is learning well. "

Gary Waddock

Histon began the second half at a frantic pace and launched the ball forward quickly and soon won a corner. A good delivery from Cambridge was met by the head of John Kennedy but his point-blank effort was smartly turned round the post by Bull.

From the resulting corner, Aldershot rushed the ball forward. A swift interchange between Hudson and Rob Elvins set up Danny Hylton but he fired wide. That quick-fire attack prompted a spell when the ball went from end to end, with Elvins and Hudson going close for Aldershot and Kennedy firing just wide for Histon.

The visitors found themselves back in the game on 63 minutes, courtesy of some classic route one football. Keeper Naisbitt launched a long kick down field and striker Murray matched Straker for pace and took advantage when the defender opted against a hoof into touch. From that, Murray was able to slot the ball past Bull, who had no chance, from the edge of the box to make the score 2-1.

With the visitors grabbing that lifeline, an air of nervousness wafted through the home fans. However, they did not have to endure the tension for too long, as the Shots scored a third within a minute. Substitute Louie Soares did well to keep the ball in play on the right and his cross into the box went straight to Hudson's feet. The in-form winger-cum-striker, who played in both positions during the game, made no mistake with another cool finish from ten yards.

From then on, Histon had most of the possession, as a corner tally of 12-3 in their favour suggests, but Aldershot were playing well within themselves and the visitors never really looked like adding another goal to their tally.

Lewis Chalmers made a welcome return after he was worryingly carried off at Torquay, and for an hour he was the man who was making things happen, along with Davies who is back to his good early-season form.

ALDERSHOT TOWN 1

(Mendes 61)

EBBSFLEET UNITED 1

(Bostwick 90)

LINE-UP

Bull, Smith (Donnelly 60), Straker, Winfield, Day, Chalmers, Soares, Harding, Mendes, Hylton (Joel Grant 55), Hudson.

> " *Ebbsfleet have to start as favourites. Any side with a two-goal lead must do.* "
>
> Gary Waddock

The likes of Bury and Grimsby may not have quite the footballing resonance of Wembley but, provided Aldershot Town can gain promotion to League Two and its plethora of northern outposts next season, then this failure to reach the home of football will quickly be forgiven, if hard to forget. Opportunities for lower league fans to watch their side at Wembley are rare; the same goes for lower league professionals and the chance to play there.

So, Aldershot's fans and players are in the same boat. There is no hiding from the fact that losing to Ebbsfleet over two legs was an opportunity missed; perhaps, even, a chance in a lifetime spurned. But, while the FA Trophy final in May would have been one of the greatest days out that the town – not just the club – had ever seen, promotion to the Football League is of far greater importance for the long-term future of the club. So now, perversely, the job is to ensure the fans and players do not have to make a different trip to Wembley this season – for the play-off final.

While Junior Mendes gave a half hour of hope, putting the Shots 1-0 up, they seldom looked like breaking down Ebbsfleet's resolute defence after that, and hopes of forcing extra time were already dying when Michael Bostwick smashed in the injury time equaliser that killed off Aldershot.

"Because you're in a semi-final of a cup, obviously you want to win it," said Waddock. "But from day one we've mentioned one thing and one thing only." And, by that, he means the league.

> " *The Trophy would have been a fantastic bonus but it didn't happen. I've said to the players in the dressing room: 'Let's just make sure that we don't feel like this come the end of April.* "

Some of the Aldershot players were close to tears at the final whistle but perhaps Louie Soares felt the worst, after a glaring miss in the 25th minute that, in a match of few chances, was to prove critical. Soares, fed by Danny Hylton, was clean through on goal, with plenty of time to decide how to beat Ebbsfleet keeper, Lance Cronin. Many of the Rec crowd expected a goal and the start of a great comeback. But anyone who saw Soares miss as many as five chances from similar positions in the Hampshire Cup exit to Basingstoke last month should have known what was coming: a weak shot and a fairly comfortable save. When it comes to shooting, Soares' confidence is shot.

With Scott Davies ill, Waddock had surprisingly favoured Soares to Joel Grant and moved Kirk Hudson to wide left. In fairness to Soares, he had enjoyed a bright opening, but after the crucial miss his confidence ebbed away and he was easily contained by Ebbsfleet's excellent left back, Sacha Opinel.

Waddock was quick to defend Soares. "You can't blame one individual. You could look at the two penalties we gave away last week or the poor defending for their third goal. It wasn't down to Louie Soares at all. He's a very good footballer."

Anthony Straker and Lewis Chalmers feel the pressure.

Waddock is right: this tie was carried away from the Shots on the wintry wind of the Thames marshes the week before, where their first half effort and concentration were poor.

Ebbsfleet defended magnificently and Waddock was quick to praise Liam Daish and his side. "Ebbsfleet made it hard for us," said Waddock. "They know we can open up teams with the way we play, so they sat deeper and deeper and made it harder and harder for us to break them down.

> *" All credit to them. They are an extremely good side and have an excellent manager. Wembley will be a fantastic experience for their football club. It's just a shame that we won't experience it. "*

On the day, too many Aldershot players could not match up their quality with their quantity of effort. Ben Harding, so important to Aldershot's fluency, was quiet again and Aldershot never gained control of the midfield, despite the best intentions and fearsome determination of Lewis Chalmers. Kirk Hudson's pace was well contained by Ebbsfleet too and perhaps, with Soares picked ahead of Grant, the Shots would have been better served with Soares on the left and Hudson on the right, which had proved effective in the second half at Ebbsfleet the week before. And Hylton struggled against Ebbsfleet's rugged and canny centre halves, Paul McCarthy and Peter Hawkins.

At least Mendes gave Ebbsfleet food for thought throughout, in an energetic display rewarded with a fine goal just after the hour. It was by far Aldershot's best move of the game and it was no surprise that Harding was at last involved. But Anthony Straker and substitutes Joel Grant and Scott Donnelly played key roles too, with Donnelly slipping in Mendes, who finished emphatically.

Donnelly did especially well in his half hour stint and must surely be pressing hard for a starting role in the league. "Junior and Scott are both good players," said Waddock. "Junior took his goal really well. Scott came on and you can see that he has a fantastic range of passing and will fit in nicely."

After the goal the Shots dominated possession but the closest they came to a goal was a cross from Grant, belatedly introduced, that just eluded Hudson. Daish had responded well to the Shots' onslaught, introducing Mark Ricketts as an extra defender and fresh legs up front, in George Purcell and Raphael Nade.

As the Shots grew more desperate even Nikki Bull came up for a corner but, in injury time, Ebbsfleet broke with pace. Bull saved superbly from Purcell but Bostwick lashed the ball home.

Ebbsfleet celebrated in style, on and off the pitch. They were Gene Kelly, singing in the rain, while the Shots were the Everly Brothers, crying in the rain.

But, all being well, the Shots will still have plenty to sing about this season.

ALDERSHOT TOWN 2
(Joel Grant 13, Straker 27)

WOKING 2
(Norville 18, Morgan 54)

(Aldershot won 4-3 on penalties, after extra time)

If Aldershot do win promotion to the Football League, Woking will miss the gate receipts from playing their near neighbours, but they will probably still be very glad to see the back of the Shots.

Four times they have played the Shots this season – and four times they have lost. This win puts Aldershot in the Setanta Shield final, after settling the match 4-3 on penalties after a 2-2 draw.

Granted, the Setanta Shield is nothing like as prestigious as the FA Trophy, and a final at Burton Albion's Pirelli Stadium (the expected venue) is not exactly Wembley Stadium. But at least this was an entertaining bounce back from Saturday's Trophy heartache against Ebbsfleet United.

Both sides enjoyed a glut of opportunities in a match that was more open than the High Street End of the Rec. Defensive purists would have been horrified, but the crowd of 1,619 were royally entertained, especially by the wing play of Aldershot's Joel Grant and Woking's Matt Pattison, a wonderful long-range goal from Anthony Straker's right foot – yes, right foot – and a penalty shoot-out that was both sublime and ridiculous.

> " *We are open and exciting with bags of pace. We create chances and concede goals. That's the way we are and we won't change.* "

The league is obviously the priority and that was reflected in Waddock's team selection. Only four of the players who started are likely to start against Altrincham at the weekend: Anthony Straker, Joel Grant, Scott Davies and Junior Mendes. Nikki Bull, Ben Harding and Lewis Chalmers were not even included in the squad and watched the fun and frolics from the stand.

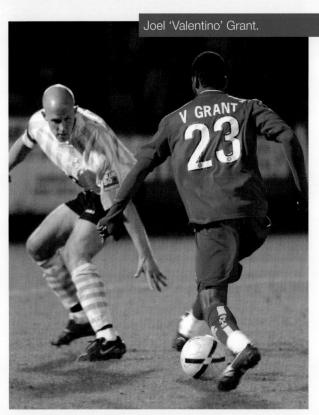
Joel 'Valentino' Grant.

So, it was little surprise that the manager was all smiles after the game; it's always nice to reach a final and this win was a nice fillip ahead of a crucial week in the league, with the Shots away three times in five days to Crawley, Droylsden and Stafford.

"I am delighted for the players and the whole club that we have made a final," said Waddock. "We have a young side and it will be a fantastic experience for them."

Aldershot's team spirit was there for all to see during the shoot-out, with the whole squad together on the touchline. "We have a close squad and lots of young lads. They want to achieve and they stick together."

Mikhael Jaimez-Ruiz saves Batt's penalty.

Those young heads largely kept their nerve in the shoot-out too, with Scott Donnelly, Davies and Kirk Hudson scoring emphatically, as did the elder statesman of the Shots, Ricky Newman. Unfortunately Grant, with a chance to seal the game, was not so cute. He had lived up to his 'non-league Ronaldo' tag in the first half, with mesmerising step-overs, shimmies and close control – plus a lovely goal to boot – but his chipped penalty made a standard back pass look like a piledriver, and was easily saved by Ross Worner.

> **❝** *I was worried when I saw Joel walking up. I could tell he might try something clever and I thought 'oh, no!' but, to be fair, he chipped in with an extremely good performance earlier.* **❞**
>
> Gary Waddock

Fortunately for Grant, the game's other outstanding player, Pattison, blasted the next kick so high it almost cleared the roof of the East Bank. But the hero of the shoot-out was Mikhael Jaimez-Ruiz, who pulled off a magnificent save to deny Damian Batt, after the seven perfect penalties that had gone before.

It was a deserved triumph for Jaimez-Ruiz, who has spent almost the entire season warming the bench as cover for Nikki Bull and deserved his moment of glory. "I'm delighted for Mikhael," said Waddock. "It was great to see him make that crucial shoot-out save."

In that first half, Woking started well but Grant gave

Aldershot the lead after a fine run in the 13th minute, set up by Mendes. Jason Norville scrambled home an equaliser five minutes later but Straker's magnificent goal made it 2-1 on 27 minutes, cutting inside from left-back and spanking a right-footed shot into the top corner.

Grant (twice), Rob Elvins, who again offered very little goal threat, and Louie Soares, who worked hard all night, might easily have extended Aldershot's advantage before half-time, but Woking were the better side after the break.

Marvin Morgan duly equalised from Pattison's cross in the 54th minute. After that, Tom Hutchinson blasted over when he should have scored and Winfield stopped the ball right on the line, after Liam Marum had rounded Jaimez-Ruiz. Seconds later the keeper denied Gray in spectacular fashion.

Both sides were tired in extra time and even Danny Hylton and Hudson, fresh from the bench, could not inspire the Shots, although they did create the best chance, with Mendes poking inches wide of the far post. There was also the uplifting sight of Ryan Scott entering the fray deep into extra time, for his first piece of competitive action against Blue Square Premier opponents since breaking his leg at the end of last season.

Such had been the entertainment on offer that referee Philips looked keen to carry on, even after Pattison had ballooned over. Hylton was called forward to take a sixth penalty, even though it wasn't necessary. Eventually the farce was sorted out and the Shots celebrated. "I was aware we had won," said Waddock. "But I'm not sure the referee was."

22 March 2008

ALDERSHOT TOWN 2
(Charles 23, Davies 67)

ALTRINCHAM 1
(Little 14)

Two moments of brilliance, from teenage midfielder Scott Davies and serial hero Nikki Bull ensured another three points for Blue Square Premier leaders Aldershot Town after a rugged encounter with Altrincham.

This script was presumably from the same book that provided the storyline for the last Saturday league match, the 2-1 victory over Kidderminster Harriers: the Shots went behind to an early goal before a cocktail of grit, determination and skill overturned the deficit against hard-working opposition determined to stifle the life out of the Shots' creative department.

However, there was an added obstacle to overcome on this occasion, with Vivaldi-inspired weather as rain, sleet, snow, wind and sun all had their turn in the spotlight to make playing conditions anything but easy. When things get difficult, though, that's when this Aldershot side simply rolls up its collective sleeves and finds a way to achieve success. It may not have been pretty for much of the game but it's results rather than performance that matter for now.

With Ben Harding starting on the left of midfield, to accommodate Davies in the centre with Lewis Chalmers, and Kirk Hudson on the right, the centre field was something of a battleground with Altrincham opting for a 4-5-1 formation. The early exchanges allowed little time or space for football.

Attacking the High Street end, the Shots had enjoyed the greater possession in the opening 13 minutes, but it was Altrincham who scored first, when a long throw from Ryan Shotton was headed across goal and top-scorer Colin Little was on the mark to side-foot home a right-footed volley.

Not surprisingly Altrincham were buoyed by taking the lead and for five minutes put the home side on the

Anthony Charles equalises.

rack. Aldershot weathered that storm (and the snow that was making another strong appearance) and on 23 minutes levelled the scores. Junior Mendes put in some deft work down the left and created enough space to place an inch-perfect low cross along the outside of the six-yard box where Anthony Charles executed a left-foot volley with precision from about eight yards out to rifle the ball home. You could feel the home supporters as a whole exhale a deep sigh of relief.

Aldershot did not create very much during the rest of the first half, and the few chances that did come their way were not dealt with clinically as the Shots had what has been a rare thing this season: a spell when they lacked a real cutting edge in front of goal.

Altrincham continued to make life difficult in the middle of the park and tried to press forward on occasions. The best chance to fall to either side in the remainder of the first 45 minutes came in time added on, as Mendes

Ben Harding enjoys the Easter weather.

sent Harding on a one-on-one with Stuart Coburn in the Altrincham goal. Unfortunately for the home side, Harding's finish from just inside the area rolled inches past the wrong side of the left-hand upright.

The second half began with Louie Soares replacing Rob Gier in the right-back roll, an attacking move by Gary Waddock as he tried to inspire his team to go on and win the game. The first 15 minutes of the half saw Aldershot having virtually all the ball, putting themselves in highly promising positions but lacking the final ball to round off the moves.

Manager Waddock decided on 54 minutes to alter his midfield make-up, with Harding moving inside to partner Chalmers in the centre, Davies going wide right and Hudson moving across to the left, while Altrincham sensed this could be their day and changed to a more adventurous 4-4-2 to match the Shots.

On 60 minutes we had the first moment of sheer brilliance; the sort of moment on which games turn and successful seasons are built. Robbie Lawton played the ball across goal from the right to find Senior just four or five yards out. He struck the ball sweetly and with power and a goal was the only possible outcome. Nikki Bull thought otherwise. Despite starting to go the other way, he changed course and blocked the ball with his raised left arm: the reaction time would have left Muhammad Ali trailing.

That moment of magic seemed to lift the Shots' players and they returned to attack mode, which earned them a free kick from 30 yards out. Davies took responsibility, grabbing the ball and firing into the top right corner of

the net while the visiting keeper was still positioning his wall. It was simply a case of quick thinking and pinpoint accuracy, which are just two of the hallmarks of Davies' season at the Rec.

With their noses now ahead for the first time in the match, Aldershot were determined to stay there and the team kept the ball well and created two or three openings without ever really looking likely to add a third goal.

> **"**It was not the best game in the world but this squad of players has shown again what great character they have to come back from a goal down. Scotty Davies will get the plaudits for his free kick but Bully's save was absolutely amazing. Obviously we would love to play free-flowing football every week, but to be honest, at this time of the season all I am interested in is the three points.**"**
>
> Gary Waddock

24 March 2008

CRAWLEY TOWN 0

ALDERSHOT TOWN 1
(Chalmers 7)

Of Aldershot's four league games in a week, this was the one that looked hardest on paper. Etching out 1-0 wins away from home, in the manner of this one, is the stuff of champions, and the three points helped the Shots go 14 points clear at the top of the Blue Square Premier. Only Torquay can catch them, and it would take a monumental collapse by the Shots for that to happen.

However, Crawley's excellent home record – ten wins and just four defeats in 18 games – was plenty for the Shots to concentrate on for this game. With captain Rhys Day carrying a knock, Gary Waddock sprung a surprise by partnering Ricky Newman with Anthony Charles in the middle of defence and sticking with Louie Soares at right-back, ahead of Rob Gier and Dean Smith.

With Waddock keen to play Ben Harding, Lewis Chalmers and Scott Davies in midfield whenever possible, Soares' chances of a start further forward look limited and he took his chance well at right-back. Only with the introduction of substitute Mustapha Carayol for the last half hour did Soares look troubled.

Then again, he was helped by a towering defensive display from Charles, ably supported by Newman. Aldershot quite simply killed the game for much of the second half, when the slanting sleet and heavy hail were more dramatic than anything the players could offer.

This was just the second time all season that Crawley have failed to score in the league at home and the first time since September. Make no mistake: keeping a clean sheet was a considerable achievement by the Shots.

As ever, they did have to rely on the excellence of Bull to see them home. Two saves in the first half were magnificent, first touching Keiran Murphy's far post header onto a post and then standing tall when the same player blasted from point-blank range, after Bull had only parried Thomas Pinault's free kick. In the second half Bull also did well to block an effort from Carayol. Even when he was stranded, Jon-Paul Pittman, headed inexplicably wide from close range.

There were the usual 'handbags' on the touchline between the management, as Martin Kuhl and counterpart Paul Raynor were sent to the stands. Crawley manager Steve Evans might easily have followed. But by the time Raynor had been banished (after 26 minutes), Aldershot had already been long in the lead. Junior Mendes earned a free kick and Harding's inswinging delivery was perfect. Chalmers escaped the attention of Lee Blackburn and headed emphatically home at the near post for his first goal for six months.

Despite surrendering plenty of possession to Crawley thereafter, Aldershot could and probably should have won by more. Mendes missed two excellent first-half chances after good passes by Joel Grant and Davies respectively, on both occasions thwarted by Bayes.

And, with eight minutes to go, Davies missed the best chance of them all, hitting a meek penalty at Bayes after substitute Rob Elvins had been hauled down in the area. Quite why Davies didn't blast the ball with customary confidence was perhaps down to Bayes, the former Leyton Orient keeper, who won the battle of minds, first delaying the kick and then dancing along his line. It was harsh on Elvins, who deserved the plaudits of setting up a goal. Even harsher was an injury time knock that threatens to sideline him, just when Danny Hylton is going off the boil.

But Aldershot held on to win the game. "We'll never play you again," sang the Aldershot hordes to the Crawley fans. Who knows, with these three points that might be true.

> **"At this stage of the season it's all about grinding out results and we've done that today."**
>
> Gary Waddock

DROYLSDEN 2

(Fearns 16, 60)

ALDERSHOT TOWN 2

(Mendes 56, Roche og 81)

LINE-UP

Bull, Soares, Straker (Day 46), Newman, Charles, Chalmers, Davies, Harding (Joel Grant 54), Mendes, Hylton (John Grant 66), Hudson.

The table-topping, ten-man Shots clinched a fortunate point at basement Droylsden, thanks to a late own goal from the home side's Lee Roche after Scott Davies had received his third red card of the season.

It was pretty grim up north for Shots fans but at least they took something from the game, in a lively 2-2 draw – just their third league stalemate of the season.

On the night, Droylsden dominated the first half and led at the break through Terry Fearns. Waddock's men were vastly improved in the second half and Junior Mendes equalised in the 57th minute, only for Fearns to restore the home side's advantage.

While this may appear an astonishing result given the gulf in points between the two sides, Gary Waddock had warned his players that there are no easy games in this division.

By twice equalising and maintaining their unbeaten league run, Waddock can rightly claim that this was a point gained, especially if the Shots can secure three points down the road in Stafford in two days' time.

Ten points from four league games in a week would still be a fantastic effort. What's more, leading goalscorer John Grant made a timely return from injury, as a second-half substitute, which is a huge boost to Waddock's squad for the last four weeks of the season.

But this was not a good performance from the league leaders, who were unsettled by Droylsden's fearless approach from the off and struggled to cope with the plucky attacking trio of Steve Denham, Fearns and Steve Daly.

Nikki Bull had already had to make three good saves when Fearns capitalised on a poor back pass from Ricky Newman and slotted the ball past Bull in the 16th minute.

The Shots were struggling to create anything – this was one of their rare away blips. But after the break, the leaders showed their resolve.

First, Junior Mendes drove a low shot from outside the area into the bottom corner, in the 56th minute, and then, after Fearns had turned in Denham's cross to restore Droylsden's lead, Louie Soares, who enjoyed a fine game as an attacking right back, forced Roche into his own-goal.

By then, it was ten plays ten at the Butcher's Arms. First Davies went for chopping down Jamie Maguire, in the 67th minute. It looked more late than malicious – just as at Grays in December – but again Davies saw red and now he faces a five-match ban. Daly followed Davies off very soon later, harshly dismissed for a challenge on Lewis Chalmers.

> **"** In my view Scott's was not a straight red card offence, but that is only my opinion and the FA panel's may differ. **"**
>
> Gary Waddock

And it was Aldershot who made the most of the extra space. Soares drove down the right and crossed low into the centre, forcing Roche to turn the ball home, to the delight of the near 300-strong Shots support, who had made the long journey to Manchester on a wild Thursday evening.

> **"** It's a testament to this side's great character and battling qualities that we came away with something from the game. **"**
>
> Gary Waddock

STAFFORD RANGERS 1
(Wellecombe 62)

ALDERSHOT TOWN 2
(Elvins 41, John Grant 65)

> **"** We weren't at our best at Droylsden but, who knows, we might be outstanding at Stafford. One thing is for sure: the team will be prepared. **"**
>
> Gary Waddock

Stafford's Marston's pedigree lost out to Aldershot's maturing vino on Saturday.

Stafford, surely heading for the Conference North, drank the bitter taste of defeat at Marston Road, while Aldershot, surely heading for the Football League, supped the sweet taste of victory, inspired by a classic first half finish by the much-maligned Rob Elvins.

> **"** That was definitely Rob's best game in an Aldershot shirt. It's good news for his confidence. **"**
>
> Gary Waddock

Elvins also had a hand in John Grant's second half winner and could easily have had a hat-trick on the day. A lack of pace and goals have not enthused Elvins to certain sections of the Aldershot faithful, but he is very popular within the squad, as the exuberant celebrations at his goal showed. "I'm delighted for Rob," said Waddock. "His hard work often goes unnoticed. It was a great move for his goal and a quality finish."

But it was Grant – in his first start for five weeks after injury – who secured another three points towards promotion to the Football League, with a header from impressive substitute Scott Donnelly's corner in the 65th minute.

This was a typical Aldershot victory: a narrow one, in which they always offered the opposition a chance of a goal but, in the end, had enough desire and creativity to score when it mattered most, just before half-time through Elvins and straight after Nick Wellecomme had headed Stafford level on 62 minutes.

With Torquay held at Altincham, Aldershot now lead the Blue Square Premier by 17 points. To be sure of promotion to the Football League, the Shots need just 11 points from their remaining seven games. And, for the more pessimistic fans, Aldershot are now definitely in the play-offs.

El Vino's vintage finish puts champagne on ice

Setanta final at the Rec

This was Aldershot's fourth league game in a week and a return of ten points is a fine achievement, especially as three of the games were away from the Recreation Ground. The three wins – over Altrincham, Crawley and Stafford – have all been narrow, but that is typical of this side. When they win games, the opposition often troop off the pitch believing that they had deserved something from the game. Stafford might argue that was the case in this match – Wellecomme headed inexplicably wide from a few yards out at 2-1 – but Aldershot created the better chances in a game played in almost impossibly windy conditions, on a boggy pitch.

After three games in five days, Waddock unsurprisingly rotated his squad and reverted, in terms of midfield and attack, to his first-choice team from the first couple of months of the season. At the back Waddock went for his most uncompromising quartet: Rhys Day and Dave Winfield in the middle and Rob Gier and Anthony Charles as full backs. Joel Grant and Anthony Straker, both key members of the squad, didn't even make the bench. "We are all about the squad," said Waddock. "After so many games we needed to keep things fresh."

Stafford won the toss and played with the fierce wind. As expected, Steve Bull's side played with a freedom and determination with which doomed sides can play against league leaders. But as the half wore on Aldershot began to create. Chalmers blasted just over, John Grant should have buried Harding's cross but headed wide from four yards out and then Danny Alcock saved well from Harding, who had been put through by Davies.

Four minutes before the break, the Shots were ahead. Soares broke superbly and slipped the ball wide to Elvins, who opened up his body and curled a right-foot shot around Alcock and into the far corner. It was a measured, composed finish of which more vaunted players who, like Elvins, lack a little pace and rely on stealth, skill and trickery – like Teddy Sheringham and Eidur Gudjohnsen – would have been proud.

Donnelly replaced the injured Davies at the break but the Shots initially struggled with the wind advantage, sending too many long, straight balls that were buffeted in no time to Alcock. That man Elvins did force Alcock into a flying save from a dipping 25-yard volley but Stafford were the side working the ball nicely, under the wind. Aldershot sat back too deep and were punished, as Wellcomme, unmarked, headed home a driven cross.

That shock awoke Aldershot from their slumber and their passing immediately improved. Elvins fed Grant and his shot was deflected inches wide. It mattered little: from Donnelly's corner, Grant headed powerfully into the roof of the net at the near post.

"We seem to be able to find that something extra just when we need to," said Waddock. "We know we can score goals and we have the confidence and belief to go and do it."

Four minutes later Wellecomme missed a very easy header but, by now, Aldershot looked like they might score every time they attacked, which was testament to their fitness after such a busy week. Charles shot just over, Grant and Elvins got in each other's way after a lovely move culminated in Donnelly's cross, and Grant shot just wide after being set up by Elvins' clever flick.

There was the odd alarm at the other end but Bull's safe hands and Day's head kept things tight while, going forward, the Shots were content to play to the corner flags, waste time and kill the game. It was hardly the style that has got them to the brink of the Football League but, at this stage of the season, points are more important than prettiness.

ALDERSHOT TOWN 3

(Mendes 71, Hudson 95, Donnelly 107)

RUSHDEN & DIAMONDS 3

(Burgess 73, 109 pen, Rankine 120)

Aldershot won 4-3 on penalties, after extra time

LINE-UP

Jaimez-Ruiz, Smith, Straker, Newman, Winfield (Gier 27), Chalmers (Harding 56), Hudson, Donnelly, John Grant (Hylton 91), Mendes, Joel Grant.

Nearly four thousand fans are probably still trying to catch their breath after a pulsating Setanta Shield final saw Aldershot squeeze past Rushden & Diamonds, 4-3 on penalties, after a 3-3 draw.

It is fitting in Gary Waddock's outstanding first season in charge that the club have won a national knockout trophy. It may not be the FA Trophy but, judging by the exuberant celebrations from players and crowd alike as the Rec reverberated in a heady evening atmosphere, the Setanta Shield certainly was a competition worth taking seriously, as Waddock has insisted all along it was. Now all he and the Shots must do is make sure that they do not have to defend their prize, by virtue of securing promotion to the Football League in the next three weeks.

"I'm delighted for the group of players – they deserve a huge amount of credit – and I'm delighted for the supporters," said Waddock afterwards.

> *" This competition has been good to us. Normally cup finals don't live up the expectation, but this one did. "*
>
> Gary Waddock

The game itself will be best remembered for an extraordinary extra time, in which there were four goals and a penalty saved. With the score at 1-1 after 90 minutes, the Shots led 3-1 at one stage but allowed Rushden back into the game in somewhat comical fashion.

But that is the Aldershot way, taking the gung-ho route to glory. The opposition is always allowed a chance to

play but in the end Aldershot had the stronger belief and will to win.

"I think tonight has been vital towards the final few weeks of the season," commented Waddock. "Losing, after putting ourselves in such a good position, may have dented the confidence a bit."

Waddock has used the Setanta Shield both to keep his side's winning momentum going through the season and to provide competitive match action for squad players and key players returning from injury and suspension. Fittingly, therefore, reserve keeper Mikhael Jaimez-Ruiz was the hero, saving Rushden's fifth penalty, from captain Chris Hope, having earlier produced an even better save to deny Andy Burgess from the spot in extra time. Granted, Jaimez-Ruiz made the odd error and was partially at fault for Michael Rankine's 120th minute equaliser but perhaps he is just fitting into the Aldershot way: triumph after making a little bit of adversity for themselves.

Scott Donnelly deserved this win more than any Aldershot player after a string of superb performances in the competition and his headed goal looked to have sealed the win at 3-1, only for even him to succumb to the madness by immediately conceding a penalty.

But perhaps the unsung star of the show was Dean Smith. He started in his favoured role at right-back but, with Dave Winfield forced off with a knee injury before the half hour, was moved in to central defence. Smith's frail frame looked unlikely to be able cope with the bulk of Rankine, however he turned in an excellent performance and with all three substitutes used, even battled on with an injury in extra time.

Kirk Hudson, however, was the man of the match on the night for Aldershot. He set up Junior Mendes' opener on

71 minutes, put the Shots 2-1 up on 95 minutes with a low shot from the edge of the area and helped Donnelly nod in the third in the 107th minute. Hudson's penalty in the shoot-out was hugely impressive too, smashing into the roof of the net.

It is testament to Waddock's squad that a player of Hudson's pace and class has been rested from league action of late. John Grant, short of match practice, started alongside Mendes up front and Hudson and Joel Grant provided the width. With Scott Davies starting a six-match ban, Waddock was always likely to pick one of Ben Harding and Lewis Chalmers with Donnelly in midfield and went with Chalmers, even if Harding, who came on just before the hour, ended up playing more minutes. Ricky Newman captained the side from central defence, with Rhys Day and Anthony Charles rested.

Mikhael Jaimez-Ruiz saves Burgess's penalty.

save from Dale Roberts, Donnelly shot inches over, Gier headed wide and Hudson was unlucky with an overhead kick.

It had been, however – as finals so often are – a pretty cagey affair. The goals took a while coming in the second half but, from the off, the game was more open. Donnelly forced a fine save from Roberts, and Mendes shot inches wide after a lovely run and pass from Joel Grant. But it was Rushden who missed the best chance; with Smith lying injured, they broke Aldershot's offside trap but Rankine was far too ponderous, having his first shot blocked and then hitting the outside of the post with the rebound.

On came Harding and the Shots immediately had a touch more poise in the midfield. But Rushden manager

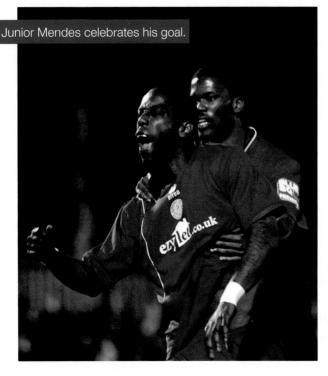
Junior Mendes celebrates his goal.

> " We were in a cup final and we wanted to win it, it was as simple as that. "
>
> Gary Waddock

The first half was a pretty drab affair and gave no indication of the thrills and spills to come. Rushden started well and, at full strength, looked the physically stronger side too. Ex-Shot Jon Challinor was finding plenty of space in the hole behind Rankine and should have done better with an excellent headed chance.

But while the Shots weren't at their best, they came closest to scoring. Lewis Chalmers forced a superb

Gary Waddock and Jaimez-Ruiz.

Ricky Newman lifts the Shield.

Two minutes into the second period of extra time, it looked all over. Hylton's shot was parried by Roberts, who then made an even better save from Hudson, but the ball ballooned up to Donnelly, who headed home.

But Hill is not a man to accept defeat and nor did his side. Substitute Abdou El-Kholti was too quick for Donnelly and Burgess showed admirable cool to step forward again, just nine minutes after missing his first penalty. He scored with aplomb. Challinor then shot wide when he should have passed and, for all Waddock's tactical changes – Mendes dropped behind Hylton and Harding sat in front of the back four – Rushden were looking the stronger side.

When Jaimez-Ruiz spilled El-Kholti's cross, Rankine hurdled the keeper and, flat on the ground, touched the grounded ball home with his nose. It was a bizarre goal, fitting for an insane period of extra time, which ended with a fine save from Jaimez-Ruiz from Tomlin's shot.

And so to penalties. Perhaps here Aldershot's home advantage finally showed. Gooding dragged the first kick wide and, with Donnelly, Harding, Newman and Hudson all scoring, the pressure mounted on Rushden. Hope's shot was weak; Jaimez-Ruiz saved; the Rec rocked as Newman and Day lifted the Shield. And now hope springs eternal that the Blue Square Premier title – and promotion – will follow shortly.

Garry Hill played a trump card too, by introducing Lee Tomlin on the right-wing. Immediately he caused problems for Anthony Straker.

It was the Shots who took the lead, when Donnelly's quick feet and surge created space and fed Hudson on the left, who crossed for Mendes to stab home his fourth goal for the club. The Shots fans were still celebrating when Rankine's long throw – at least he was effective in that respect – into the box caused havoc and Burgess turned the ball home. Rushden should then have gone on to win the final in normal time, only for Rankine to head wide in injury time from just a few yards out. It was an extraordinary miss and would eventually prove decisive.

Waddock refreshed his troops with the introduction of Danny Hylton, in place of John Grant, for extra time. Rankine missed another good chance before Hudson restored Aldershot's lead, shooting into the near corner after a sideways run across the edge of the area.

Rushden should have drawn level just five minutes later, when Gier was adjudged to have fouled Andy Gooding in the box. Aldershot were furious – Challinor had looked yards offside seconds before – but it mattered little, as Jaimez-Ruiz dived to his left to hold onto Burgess's penalty.

We've installed a winning mentality, which comes from confidence and belief. Now we must remain in that frame of mind and pick up as many points as possible between now and the end of the season.

Gary Waddock

DAYS THINKS IT ALL OVER

4 April 2008

I think a few of the lads were a bit disappointed that we couldn't go out and celebrate winning the Setanta Shield last night. But that was never going to happen with the league game against Salisbury to come so soon afterwards. There is still plenty of work to be done. Do that and we can hopefully all have a huge celebration in a few weeks' time.

The way the fans celebrated last night's win has made us even more determined to go and finish the main job in the league. The way we felt last night, the smiles on all the lads' faces and the cheers of the fans...just imagine what they will be like if we win the league.

It really was an excellent crowd last night. I know the players want success and it just shows how much the fans want it too. It was a late finish last night but the fans stayed until after the end, even though I guess plenty of them had to get up this morning as early as 5am or 6am to get to work.

I must admit that when we went 3-1 up I thought it was done and dusted, but as soon as they got back to 3-2 then I knew it might be a dodgy five minutes, and so it proved. But once we got to penalties, I fancied us. I didn't think any of our guys would miss and they didn't.

The Setanta Shield is pretty big so captain on the night Ricky Newman said to me he might need a hand lifting it. Actually, we called Bully [Nikki Bull] up too, as I guess we are the three senior players in the squad. But Bully said "that's not for me, as I haven't played in the competition at all," so he left us two to it.

I think Mikhael [Jaimez-Ruiz] has been brilliant in his attitude all season. You're never going to get much change out of Bully, he's the best keeper in non-league football by a street. And he's pretty unbreakable, he's barely been injured for six years at Aldershot. But it shows the strength we've got that we have Mikhael to come in when selected. He's a class act and it was great he made the winning save and celebrated with the fans.

It's the first time I've lifted a trophy in first team football.

I won a few things in reserve and youth football with Manchester City but they just don't compare to winning something at senior level, like last night. It certainly makes me want to go on and lift some more silverware.

Unfortunately Dave Winfield picked up a knee injury last night. He was having a scan this afternoon, so we'll have to see how he is. But the majority of the boys are OK after last night and the attitude in training today was excellent.

All year the gaffer has made sure that all we do is concentrate on the next game. But obviously we are all aware of the situation and what we need to finish top. It's at the back of our minds, yes, but we know that the best way of going about things is by getting as many points as we can, as soon as possible. Starting tomorrow against Salisbury. It will be a tough game: they all are in this league, as Droylsden and Stafford showed us last week. We may have beaten Salisbury 4-0 away in December but for me that was never a '4-0 game'. They are a very decent team.

I didn't think Scott Davies' tackle at Droylsden was worthy of a red card, but I think his previous suspension record counted against him at the appeal. To be honest, however, his ankle is not looking good and is very swollen. I don't think he'd have played for a couple of weeks anyway. He has a heel injury too, which requires an operation, which may well be brought forward now. That way, hopefully he will decide to stay with us and will be fully fit for pre-season for next season.

It was nice to have Jonny Dixon back at the Recreation Ground to watch last night's final. He had no commitments with Brighton and rang me to see if there was a ticket for the final. He came into the dressing room for 10-15 minutes to say hi. He remains a massive part of this season for us and will always be welcome back here.

We had a good 'road trip' up north last week and picked up a good few points. I was rooming with my old mate Anthony Charles again, so I spent as much time out of the room as possible. Hopefully we may be able to enjoy a proper 'road trip' and celebration, courtesy of the club, once the season is over. But we have a league to win first.

5 April 2008

ALDERSHOT TOWN 2
(Elvins 3, Hylton 82)

SALISBURY CITY 1
(Feeney 61)

> *"A lot of people away from the club are saying that we are already champions. But we are not. There are no free points in this league. Salisbury have had a great first season in the Conference and, as they can't go up and down, will play with confidence and freedom. Everyone expects us to get the three points; but all we can really do is keep doing what we've been doing."*
>
> Nikki Bull

Come tomorrow tonight (Tuesday), Aldershot may be back in the Football League.

After this typically narrow victory and Torquay's shock defeat at home to Farsley Celtic, Aldershot are 17 points clear and need just five points from the last six games to be crowned Blue Square Premier champions – and with it, win promotion to the Football League. But, should the Shots win at Ebbsfleet United's Stonebridge Road ground tomorrow and Torquay fail to beat Oxford United at home, the Shots will be up.

There would be a certain catharsis, should the Shots achieve their season-long aim at Stonebridge Road, given that their FA Trophy dreams were all but dashed at Ebbsfleet last month. But it matters little. Whenever, wherever, the Shots are going up. Even the most pessimistic of Shots fans must no longer feel guilty by contemplating the Football League. Next season, when

they play against one of England's foremost cathedral cities, it will be Lincoln, not Salisbury.

But while it is the Shots who stand tall at the top of Blue Square Premier – their lead is nearly as high as the spire of Salisbury Cathedral itself – there was little to indicate on Saturday that they were the superior team, heading to the Football League.

Salisbury City left the Rec unlucky to lose after a plucky second half display that, for a while, had the Shots on the ropes. But Salisbury merely join a long list of sides who have left this corner of Hampshire feeling aggrieved after a narrow league defeat: Rushden & Diamonds, Grays Athletic, Stafford Rangers, Woking, Kidderminster Harriers – the list goes on.

Indeed, this victory was so typically Aldershot. The brilliance of keeper Nikki Bull was ultimately critical, before the Shots' self-belief and winning mentality proved triumphant. Aldershot have the best keeper in

The Shots celebrate Hylton's winner.

Nikki Bull was crucial to the Shots' 2-1 victory.

of taking off right-back Rob Gier for a forward, Danny Hylton.

And the two new players were at the heart of the Shots' winning goal, with just eight minutes left on the clock. Hylton's darting run was ended by a trip by Salisbury captain Aaron Cook. Donnelly floated over the free kick, Anthony Charles headed back across goal and Hylton headed into the roof of the net. Cue bedlam around the Rec.

But at times the afternoon had been far from comfortable for the Shots. They were gifted an early lead when, after Salisbury had dominated the opening exchanges, the visitors' defence inexplicably misjudged Anthony Straker's fairly hopeful long pass and, to compound their ineptitude, left Elvins unmarked on the penalty spot.

Elvins brought the ball down expertly and his confident, if straightforward, finish in front of the East Bank, boosted his morale even further following last week's goal at Stafford. The goals, like El Vino, are beginning to flow, now that he's been uncorked.

But Aldershot looked fairly flat in an uninspiring first half. That said, Hudson, who enjoyed another good game, and John Grant, who continues to work back to full fitness, had good efforts on target early on, and Hudson then hit the post, beating Clarke at his near post with very little backlift, from the edge of the area.

Salisbury looked increasingly dangerous as the second half developed, even if Aldershot had the better chances. Soares – all too familiarly – shot high and wide when through and then Hudson pounced on an error from Clarke, after Cook's back pass, but, off-balance, shot into the side stanchion rather than the empty net. Two minutes later Salisbury were level, as Feeney smashed in a rebound after a good save from Bull. News filtered through that Comply Or Die had won the Grand National at Aintree. But Salisbury were doing neither and looked the more likely winners. Tubbs volleyed over when well placed and Rob Sinclair was inches away from a low cross.

The best chance fell to substitute Ashley Barnes, who was superbly thwarted by Bull's point-blank save in the 77th minute. Two minutes later Feeney wasted another glorious opening.

In fairness, the Shots were impressive going forward too in the second half. John Grant lobbed inches wide after good work by Anthony Straker and the midfield axis of Harding-Donnelly-Hudson worked fluently. Eventually, Hylton's presistence paid off and the Shots had, yet again, done just enough to gain another win.

the division and score plenty of goals. Together, that has added up to a string of wins all season.

Saturday's was Aldershot's 30th league win of the season, which means they have taken maximum points from three-quarters of their games. Gary Waddock's mantra: "We take one game at a time and always look to win the three points," has proved simple but successful.

Two substitutes changed the course of the match, so Waddock and Martin Kuhl must take credit for that too. Soon after Salisbury's Liam Feeney had cancelled out Rob Elvins' early opener, Waddock swapped Lewis Chalmers for Scott Donnelly in midfield and, while 1-1 would have been a perfectly adequate result in the circumstances, the manager made the bold move

8 April 2008

EBBSFLEET UNITED 2
(Moore 14, McPhee 88)

ALDERSHOT TOWN 2
(John Grant 56, 71)

It is said that good things come to those who wait. So, Aldershot and their fans just need to be patient, after the results required for promotion to the Football League did not happen on Tuesday evening.

For a few tantalising minutes – seven, to be precise – it appeared that Stonebridge Road, home of Ebbsfleet United, would be the venue for Aldershot's historic return to where they belong, in the Football League. John Grant had just put the Shots 2-1 up and Torquay were being held 1-1 at home to Oxford. Had things stayed that way, the Shots would be up. But Torquay, who had trailed to a first-minute goal, came back to win 3-2 and were ahead by the time former-Shot Chris McPhee swept in a deserved equaliser for Ebbsfleet.

While the manner of conceding a late equaliser was a kick in the teeth for Gary Waddock and his players, the manager was quick to accentuate the positives of another point gained. A draw at Ebbsfleet United, in normal circumstances, is a fair result. After all, just look what happened to the Shots at Stonebridge Road last month in the FA Trophy semi-final: a 3-1 defeat.

"This is a difficult place to come to," said Waddock. "We were leading with two minutes to go and it would have been great to get the three points.

> **"** *A point away from home, it doesn't matter where you are, is a good point. Especially here.* **"**

Given how many games Aldershot have won by just the odd goal in the league this season – 20 – and the somewhat fortuitous nature of several of those wins, the Shots could have few complaints with Ebbsfleet's equaliser, even if it came so late in the day.

"I think it was a fair reflection," said Waddock. "At 2-1 we had chances to kill the game off but, then again, Bully [Nikki Bull] has made a number of good saves, yet again."

Bull made an astonishing double save from Neil Barrett in the first half – the offside flag went up for the second shot, but Bull was not to know – and, three minutes before McPhee's late goal, Bull denied the game's outstanding player, Stacey Long, in a one-on-one situation.

Luke Moore hit the side-netting after rounding Bull in the second half and Ben Harding blocked a goalbound shot: Ebbsfleet were good value for their two goals. While Anthony Charles had another commanding performance at the back, captain Rhys Day, out with a minor leg injury, was missed alongside him. Dave Winfield is injured too, so Ricky Newman came in and was given a testing evening by an Ebbsfleet attack missing Chukki Eribenne and John Akinde, who had caused the Shots so many problems in the Trophy.

But it was out wide where the Shots struggled most. Long tormented Rob Gier in the Trophy game at Stonebridge and it was another uncomfortable evening for the right-back. Ebbsfleet's opening goal, after 14 minutes, turned in by Moore, came from a cross from Gier's side.

And, on the left of defence, Anthony Straker failed to settle and he was partly to blame for McPhee's equaliser, caught up field. But credit must got to McPhee too, for a flashing finish, high into the roof of Bull's net.

By the end, Aldershot were walking wounded, with both Harding and Soares carrying cut lips, Chalmers hobbling with a hamstring problem and Scott Donnelly only getting up gingerly from a heavy challenge right on the final whistle.

"We picked up some knocks tonight," said Waddock. "We haven't got the biggest squad in the world and there's a big game to come on Saturday." Chalmers must be a huge doubt for the Burton match – he looks set to be suspended for the Exeter and Halifax games after picking up a tenth booking of the season – but the good news is that Day is expected to be fit tomorrow.

Even better news is the return to full fitness of John Grant. In a glorious 15-minute period in the second half the Shots turned the game on its head – thanks to Grant's head.

Twice he was johnny-on-the-spot to claim classic poacher's goals. First, in the 56th minute, after Louie Soares had headed Kirk Hudson's cross against the bar, Grant dived first to the rebound to beat keeper Lance Cronin.

Then, in the 71st minute, after good work by Rob Elvins and substitute Joel Grant, Chalmers cushioned a header back across goal and Grant dived in for another close-range header.

> " *It was an open game, it always is with us. But it sets it up for the weekend and I am already looking forward to it.* "
>
> Gary Waddock

How they rated

Nikki Bull
Made series of super saves and more comfortable with crosses than of late. (8)

Rob Gier
Started slowly but was increasingly impressive. As hard in the tackle as ever. (7)

Anthony Straker
Prone to the occasional error but made a number of vital interceptions. (7)

Anthony Charles
Very solid at the back and dominant in the air, especially in after the break. (7)

Rhys Day
Led by example in tricky conditions for defenders. Dangerous at set pieces. (8)

Ben Harding
Great composure for his goal and was a little unlucky not to score more. (8)

Lewis Chalmers
Back to his biting best in the middle and had a hand in all the goals too. (8)

Louie Soares
Good, hard-working return after injury, even if stop not in top gear. (7)

John Grant
STAR MAN. Three wonderful goals, showing power, composure and deft touch. (9)

Jonny Dixon
Should have scored in the first half but full marks for hard work and energy. (7)

Joel Grant
Salisbury looked worried whenever he got the ball. Shows super touch and balance. (8)

SUBS: Newman, 6, Elvins 7, Hudosn 6. Subs not used: Jaimez-Ruiz, Smith.

Gary Waddock remains fully focused as the Shots edge closer to the Football League.

Waddock made to wait as Fleet halt promotion push

IT is said that good things come to those who wait.

So, Aldershot and their fans just need to be patient, after the results required for promotion to the Football League did not happen on Tuesday evening.

For a few tantalising minutes – seven – it appeared that Stonebridge Road, home of Ebbsfleet United, would be the venue for Aldershot's historic return to where they belong, in the Football League.

John Grant had just put the Shots 2-1 up and Torquay were being held 1-1 at home to Oxford. Had things stayed that way, the Shots would be up.

First doing Ebbsfleet International, next stop the Football League.

But Torquay, who had rallied to a first-minute equal, came back to win 3-2 and soon ahead by the time former-Shot Chris McPhee swept in a deserved equaliser for Ebbsfleet.

Now, the Shots must look to finish the job at home to Burton Albion tomorrow (Saturday), depending on how Torquay do on their trip to Stevenage.

But, don't be surprised if, to be absolutely certain, the Shots will need something from the away trip next Tuesday to Exeter City or, even, the Saturday afternoon at Halifax Town.

While the pressure of controlling a late equaliser was a kick in the teeth for Gary Waddock and his players, the manager was quick to accentuate the positives of another point gained. A draw at Ebbsfleet United, in normal circumstances, is a fine result.

After all, just look what happened in the Shots at Stonebridge Road last month in the FA Trophy semi-final: a 3-1 defeat.

"This is a difficult place to come to," said Waddock. "We were looking with two minutes to go and it would have been great to get the three points.

"But a point away from home, is doesn't matter where you are, is a good point. Especially here."

Louie Soares takes on Burton in the 2-0 defeat in October.

Vital Rec clash — for both sides

WHEN Aldershot were comfortably beaten — 2-0 at Burton Albion in October, it didn't seem likely then for the seven-game, just a fortnight before the last match of the season, the Shots would be 15 points clear at the top and requiring a maximum of four points to guarantee promotion to the Football League.

The Shots's powerful position puts the failure to take maximum points from Tuesday's trip to Ebbsfleet United into perspective. They are still in a wonderful situation and Tuesday's draw was another point towards promotion.

However, had Chris McPhee not prodded back the Shots late on, they would have gone into tomorrow's match against Burton in the knowledge that a win would have guaranteed promotion. Now, for that to happen tomorrow, Torquay must slip up. If the Shots get a better result than Torquay, who face a tricky trip to Stevenage on Tuesday, its fourth-placed and play-off chasing Stevenage Borough, they are up.

So, if the Shots win, a draw or loss for Torquay will mean they cannot catch Gary Waddock's side. Likewise, if Aldershot draw and Torquay lose, the Shots are up. If such sides get the same result then Torquay could, conceivably, still overhaul the Shots on goal difference.

All the permutations matter little to Waddock, however.

"People can talk about its, buts and maybes but all I'm concerned about are points. Let's see how many we have by the end of the season."

Burton are in desperate need of points too. One of them, Exeter, Cambridge and Stevenage look set to miss out on a play-off spot, although Nigel Clough's side gave themselves a great boost with a last-minute winner from John Brayford at home to Mtrrosham on Tuesday, while Exeter lost at Salisbury. Before that, Burton had lost two games on a row against Grays and Forest Green Rovers.

"It's all set for a hell of a game," said Waddock. "There should be a big crowd and a fantastic atmosphere. They are looking for points for one reason; we want them for another. All we can do is look for three points."

Captain Rhys Day is expected to return to the starting line-up, while Louie Soares may start at right-back, with Joel Grant pushing for a recall in midfield. Should Lewis Chalmers be ruled out with a hamstring injury, Waddock has a replacement in Scott Donnelly.

Kick-off at the Rec is 3pm.

Ebbsfleet United 2
Aldershot Town 2
Blue Square Premier
by Charlie Oliver at Stonebridge Road
Match rating: ✗✗✗ Attd: 1,439
Referee: J Scarr

TOP OF BLUE SQUARE PREMIER

	P	W	D	L	GD	Pts
Aldershot T	41	30	8	3	53	98
Torquay U	42	24	7	11	32	79
Cambridge U	42	22	11	9	22	77
Stevenage B	42	22	7	13	14	74
Burton A	41	21	11	9	23	74
Exeter C	41	19	15	7	21	72

Match Facts

	Salis	Shots
Shots on target	6	11
Shots off target	6	4
Corners	12	6
Caught offside	9	4
Fouls committed	10	8
Yellow Cards	1	3
Red Cards	0	0

The News, 11 April 2008.

12 April 2008

ALDERSHOT TOWN 1
(Elvins 36)

BURTON ALBION 0

Football teams rarely make things easy for their loyal supporters and Saturday was no exception for the Aldershot faithful.

Yet again the Shots won – a record 31st Conference victory of the season, taking them to 97 points – but this, especially in the first half, was too often a nervous, patchy and lethargic performance. As so often, the skills of keeper Nikki Bull were the difference between three points and very possibly none, although the wayward finishing of Burton Albion's Shaun Harrad helped Aldershot no end too.

From the off, the bumper crowd of nearly 6,000 was fairly subdued. Perhaps most in the ground had already guessed that this would not be the day of Aldershot's resurrection back to the Football League. And so it proved: Aldershot needed to better Torquay's result at Stevenage Borough to clinch promotion. Just as at Ebbsfleet last Tuesday evening, results were going Aldershot's way after Rob Elvins' 36th minute header at the Rec, but the Gulls did not play ball at Broadhall Way, coming from behind to win 3-1.

But on the day, Aldershot did what they had to do and now require just one point from four remaining games. At this stage of the season the manner of victory is irrelevant. Championships are won by points picked up when a side is not at their best; it is all about the three points, as a certain flame-haired manager might say.

Besides, this was typical Aldershot. Winning by the odd goal is de rigueur for their season – 21 of their 31 victories have come in this manner – and the Shots are certainly back in fashion, judging by the national media presence at the Rec on Saturday.

Waddock was unsurprisingly very happy in victory and typically honest in his assessment of a tough game for his side. "I'm delighted with the result," said Waddock. "We rode our luck, but you need a little bit of luck to win anything. When all is said and done we have kept a clean sheet and got the three points."

Rob Elvins had plenty to shout about.

❝ All we can do is pick up points and results. We can't affect results elsewhere. But now that we need one point from four games, it is in our hands. ❞

Gary Waddock

Burton had outplayed the Shots in a 2-0 victory at the Pirelli Stadium in October and did likewise for much of this game, despite Nigel Clough choosing to rest key striker Daryl Clare. Had Clare played, the result may well have been different.

Burton is famous for being tasty – beer, Bovril, Branston's Pickle and Marmite all hail from the banks of the Trent – and their football gave Aldershot's creaky defence, again missing injured captain Rhys Day, plenty of food for thought.

Burton's passing and movement was crisp and incisive and gave Waddock's side a taste of their own medicine. Burton are, after all, taught by Clough and Gary Crosby, two star scholars of the football academy that Clough's late father, Brian, ran at Nottingham Forest. But, on the day, how they could have done with the clinical finishing Clough Junior enjoyed as a player at Forest.

In the first half, Marc Goodfellow headed wide of a gaping goal and Jake Edwards scooped inches over. Bull made two good blocks, as did Anthony Straker, Aldershot's best defender on the day. On the stroke of half-time Harrad, clean through, with time and space at his disposal, was denied by Bull's fingertips, even if referee Kinseley, who was pedantic throughout, awarded a goal kick.

Aldershot had created nothing going forward for the first half hour, and it was little wonder that coach Martin Kuhl barked out: "We've got to start playing," at his listless players. Finally Straker supplied much-needed energy and almost burst clear from left-back, after a one-two with Louie Soares. A minute later, completely against the run of play, Elvins headed the Shots ahead from Joel Grant's cross, with his third goal in four games.

The Shots were far more potent going forward in the second half, especially after the introduction of Hudson with 25 minutes to go, and at least created a series of chances. But it was Burton who continued to enjoy the best of them.

Harrad was clean through again on 47 minutes but his touch let him down. He then shot just wide, this time under pressure from Ricky Newman, before smacking the inside of Bull's near post in the 75th minute. In injury time Bull saved superbly with his feet from substitute Matt Williams, after Anthony Charles, not for the first time, fell over. When Burton finally did get the ball in the net, Darren Stride's finish was ruled out by an offside flag. The Rec breathed a collective sigh of relief; Bull blew a kiss at the referee's assistant.

Soares, Hudson and Elvins all went close for the Shots in the second half but it wouldn't really be Aldershot if they had opened up a two-goal lead. After all, this side prefers a narrow win – and this one was as narrow as they come.

The good news is that Aldershot don't need another win; all that is needed now is just one more point. And, with Bull in goal, it will happen.

DAYS THINKS IT ALL OVER

14 April 2008

We were obviously disappointed the Torquay result on Saturday meant that our win over Burton was not enough to give us the title and promotion. But now we need just one point from four games. And, if we can't get that point across that many games, then we simply don't deserve to go up.

The boys had to dig in against Burton and Bully made a couple of good saves again. The boy Shaun Harrad hit the post in the second half. How he missed that I really don't know. But that's what wins you championships, a little bit of luck like that.

It was a nightmare having to watch from the stand. I said to Gary Waddock afterwards, "We could have done with winning that a little more easily than we did," but it was an exciting game to watch and we got the three points, which is all that matters.

We're all really pleased for Rob Elvins. His contribution has been massive since he came back into the side recently, after not really getting much of a look-in for a

while. It's brilliant for him and the team and there he was with the winner again on Saturday.

I've been ill as well as injured and the illness has been getting me down. But I've got a prescription from the doctor so hopefully the medicine will sort that one out. And hopefully, if I keep icing up my knee, I should be fit for Exeter on Tuesday and, if not, Halifax on Saturday.

The games this week away are going to be very difficult. Exeter need the points to make the play-offs and Halifax are fighting for their lives near the bottom. But hopefully we'll get that point – if not more – at Exeter.

We all plan to watch the reserve game against Queens Park Rangers at the Rec on Monday afternoon and then travel down to Exeter together, to get the three points. Everyone is very excited. I want to be playing. And, if we do win the title at Exeter I want to be there, in my kit, sweating after 90 minutes, not coming on in my suit, that's for sure.

EXETER CITY 1
(Stansfield 39)

ALDERSHOT TOWN 1
(Donnelly 42)

LINE-UP
Bull, Gier, Straker, Newman, Charles, Donnelly, Soares, Harding, John Grant, Elvins, Hudson.

Exeter is a city of saints – and on Tuesday night a new saint was anointed in the city. Saint Gary.

The Cathedral Church of Saint Peter is steeped in history and Exeter St David's railway station was designed by none other than Isambard Kingdom Brunel. But on Tuesday night at St James' Park, home to Exeter City, Gary Waddock and his Aldershot team made history.

Aldershot football is back where it belongs: in the Football League. Sixteen years after league status died with the old Aldershot FC, Waddock, backed to the hilt by players, the board and backroom staff alike, has taken Aldershot Town to the Promised Land and Aldershot football back to its spiritual home. Come next season the Shots will once again be members of the celestial body that is the '92 Club', which makes up the Football League.

Non-league football has been a very happy hunting ground for the Shots and fond memories abound but now they move on to bigger and – hopefully – better things. Those fans who watched the old club in the Football League know that Aldershot football is back where it ought to be. So, it's goodbye to Farsley Celtic and Droylsden and hello to the likes of Brentford and Luton Town.

Torquay United, hoping that Aldershot would suffer a collapse as dramatic as Devon Loch's infamous stumble in the 1956 Grand National, did all they could, winning 1-0 at home to Northwich Victoria. That meant, for the Shots to win the title and promotion on the night, they had to gain a draw or better, 20 miles to the east. And it was more a case of Devon unlock than Devon Loch, as Scott Donnelly's first half equaliser ensured that Waddock and the Shots have the keys to League Two.

Stiff challenges lie ahead – many of them in the north – and Waddock will certainly not allow himself or his squad to rest on their laurels. But for now they can enjoy the moment and bask in a magnificent achievement.

"It is absolutely fantastic," said Waddock after the game, in a rare moment when he wasn't embracing his players and dancing on the terrace with the ecstatic Aldershot hordes who had made the trip to the South West.

"But work never stops. We will enjoy the moment and then get busy planning for the future."

Bookmakers Victor Chandler are already looking ahead to next season and are quoting odds as low as 4-1 for Aldershot to win back-to-back promotions. So, expectations are high.

But, to most Aldershot fans, even this promotion appeared highly unlikely when Waddock was installed as manager last May, replacing Terry Brown.

The Shots had finished ninth and 13th in the Conference in the last two seasons under Brown, after reaching the play-off final and semi-final respectively in seasons 2003-04 and 2004-05, and a year of consolidation and no more was expected under Waddock.

One man thought differently, however: Waddock. The Waddock factor should not be underestimated and it's impossible to speak to a member of the Aldershot squad without hearing praise for his man-management skills and Martin Kuhl's coaching and motivational expertise.

"The Waddock/Kuhl partnership will go to the very top of the game," said goalkeeper Nikki Bull, amid the champagne and celebrations.

"The Gaffer came in and sat back and assessed and let Martin get on with the coaching. He worked out our strengths, weaknesses and the players' characters, and pieced it all together.

> " The Gaffer has an aura about him. The players would run through a brick wall for him. "
>
> Nikki Bull

This was the first game that Aldershot's destiny was in their own hands. Forget Torquay, their result was irrelevant provided the Shots finished their own job.

Typically, they did it, as Waddock's side almost always does. Normally, the goal is three points but, just this once, only needing the one point, Waddock's men did the job all the same.

As usual, too, it was a close shave. Aldershot rarely make viewing easy for the fans and as the second half wore on, Waddock's men sat deeper as they edged closer towards the final whistle.

Exeter, desperate for three points to boost their bid for a play-off spot, poured forward, especially after the introduction of Wayne Carlisle on the right, but the Shots' defence stood firm.

Anthony Charles was outstanding and Ricky Newman, who kept his place in the absence of injured and ill captain Rhys Day, used all his experience to marshal the backline.

The dramatic circumstances of the game ensured that it was captivating viewing but only a handful of key moments were of consequence for the Shots.

First, against the run of play, after Aldershot had made a bright start, Adam Stansfield burst on to Matthew Gill's astute pass and swept the home side into a 39th minute lead.

As so often this season, Waddock's side raised their game as circumstances dictated and, vitally, were on level terms before the break.

John Grant held the ball up well and his square pass was perfectly placed for Donnelly to shoot on target. Veteran goalkeeper Andy Marriott should have saved what was no more than a firm shot, but mistimed his dive and helped the ball into the net. Cue bedlam on the away terrace and a far more buoyant away dressing room at half-time than it might have been.

It was Donnelly's first league goal for the Shots on his first start. "It was just nice to start," he said afterwards. "But fantastic to get the goal.

"I haven't been here in the first team long but I feel I've played my part tonight."

Donnelly's set-piece expertise troubled Exeter all night and Kirk Hudson, Louie Soares and Charles all missed good chances that would have eased the Shots' nerves in the second half. But it was the other end that mattered: if Bull could keep a second half clean sheet, then the Shots were up.

Bull made a superb save from Dean Moxey's flying header on the hour and the rebound ricocheted inches

Nikki Bull
Magnificent late save ensured the Shots are not still waiting nervously.
8

Rob Gier
Solid game at right back. Coming good again after a slight dip in form.
7

Anthony Straker
Comfortable first half but tested once Exeter added more width on the right. 6

Anthony Charles
STAR MAN Should have scored but in main job, at the back, he was superb. 8

Ricky Newman
Used all his experience to keep Exeter at bay as they pushed for winner. 7

Ben Harding
Back to his best. Sublime passing set up series of chances and attacks. 8

Scott Donnelly
Perfect time to score first league goal and enjoyed impressive full league debut. 7

Louie Soares
Finishing and final ball let him down but was full of important running. 6

John Grant
Set up goal and led the line well, especially when isolated in second half. 7

Rob Elvins
Tireless work helped keep Exeter on back foot, especially in first half. 6

Kirk Hudson
Started superbly and pace worried Exeter but was guilty of wasting chances. 7

Match Facts

	Ex	Shots
Shots on target	6	6
Shots off target	1	9
Corners	1	7
Caught offside	2	1
Fouls committed	9	8
Yellow Cards	1	1
Red Cards	0	0

TOP OF BLUE SQUARE PREMIER

	P	W	D	L	GD	Pts
Aldershot T	43	31	5	7	34	98 *
Torquay U	42	26	7	9	30	85
Burton A	43	22	11	10	23	77
C'bridge U	43	22	11	10	21	77
Stevenage B	43	23	7	13	30	76
Exeter C	43	20	16	7	20	76

* Champions and promoted

❏ ALDERSHOT are away to struggling Halifax Town tomorrow (Saturday) in the Blue Square Premier. Kick-off is at 3pm.

---

wide off Newman. Deep into the last ten minutes, Exeter were adamant that Bull had fouled Stansfield in the area but referee Sarginson waved play on and Aldershot fans breathed again.

But no Aldershot game appears to pass without a Bull wonder save and his superb, one-handed dive to pull back Steve Basham's 87th minute header from behind him was a microcosm of Aldershot's title and promotion triumph: the outfield players have laid the foundations but it's Bull's hands that have helped most towards building a total close to 100 points.

Afterwards, Bull was typically modest. "Saves are instinctive, you don't really think about saves until you've actually made them."

> **" Besides, this has all been about the squad. We win and lose as a squad. "**

And they celebrate as a squad too – along with the management, fans, backroom staff and directors. For an hour after the final whistle, St James' Park became a little corner of Aldershot. And the last words are best left to the fans. Altogether now: "Going up to the Football League..."

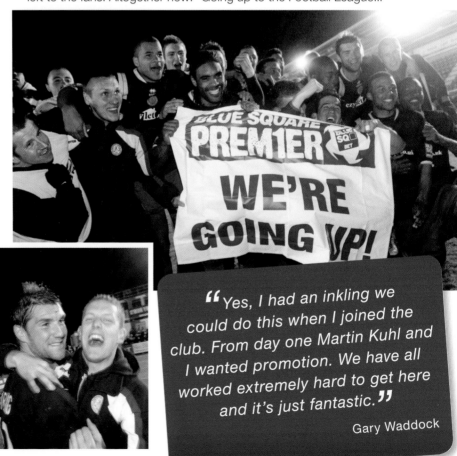

> **" Yes, I had an inkling we could do this when I joined the club. From day one Martin Kuhl and I wanted promotion. We have all worked extremely hard to get here and it's just fantastic. "**
>
> Gary Waddock

HALIFAX TOWN 0

ALDERSHOT TOWN 0

LINE-UP

Jaimez-Ruiz, Gier, Straker, Newman, Charles, Donnelly, Harding, Scott (Joel Grant 56), Williams (Hudson 56), John Grant, Rob Elvins (Hylton 83).

There may have been no goals during Aldershot Town's visit to the Shay, but there was plenty of end-to-end action and goalmouth thrills during this encounter with Halifax Town that could just as easily have seen the two sides sharing eight goals.

Just one note of criticism was that a particularly bumpy pitch did not make things easy for either side to get the ball down and play, but that makes it even more praiseworthy that an entertaining game was put on for spectators by both teams.

Gary Waddock picked a team that included long-term absentees Ryan Williams and Ryan Scott, who have both endured a nightmare time through serious injury, while the manager also handed a league debut to goalkeeper Mikhael Jaimez-Ruiz. It was the first time since April 2004 that Nikki Bull has not been in an Aldershot Town league line-up, which is the small matter of 178 matches.

The newly-crowned Blue Square Premier champions were taking on a Halifax side fighting against the threat of relegation, although Halifax have only been plunged into that situation by a ten-point deduction for going into administration. Having shown their respects to the Shots when they formed a guard of honour for the visitors as they came on to the field of play, Halifax forgot all about reputations during the game as they came out of the traps like a fast-starting Wimbledon track specialist.

Mind you, for all the possession Halifax enjoyed during the first 20 minutes, there were not many clear-cut chances on goal other than three or four long-range efforts that never looked likely to trouble Jaimez-Ruiz.

In those opening exchanges the Shots looked a little disjointed, although Williams was always lively and went close with a 20-yard free kick, while Ben Harding ghosted in on 30 minutes to glance a header just wide of the upright as a trademark Shots break caught the home defence during a momentary lapse of concentration.

The home side continued their almost gung-ho approach and in the final ten minutes of the opening half almost laid siege to the Aldershot goal. Twice Jaimez-Ruiz pulled off cracking saves, from a close-range effort by Jon Shaw (when it looked long odds-on that he would score) and a sharp shot by Tom Kearney.

It was not just Jaimez-Ruiz who was playing his part in the defensive display, though, and the back four were all putting in determined performances. None more so than right-back Rob Gier who was tackling, intercepting and closing down as if his life depended on it. In addition, midfielder Scott Donnelly tracked back with a responsibility that belied his tender years.

The second half began pretty much like the first 45 had begun, with Halifax in the driving seat and Shaw and Lewis Killeen, who has always seemed to raise his game against the Shots, making themselves a real nuisance but they were unable to find a way to outwit the inspired Jaimez-Ruiz. When Shaw did manage to place a 52nd minute header beyond the reach of the keeper, Ricky Newman was in the right place at the right time to make a goal-line clearance.

Waddock decided to make a bold switch on 56 minutes, taking off Scott and Williams and introducing Kirk Hudson and Joel Grant. And within a matter of minutes, both of these attacking-orientated substitutes could have made Halifax pay for their profligacy in front of goal.

Joel Grant found himself denied by Legzdins (on loan from Birmingham City) when unleashing a side-footed volley from five yards, while Hudson lost out to the keeper when shooting a few minutes later. The Shots were now showing glimpses of the pace, power and precision that has made this such a successful campaign.

However, Halifax still had the resolve to do anything but roll over and let the champions swamp them. The Shaymen came forward again as the game switched ends regularly as the tempo was cranked up.

During the final half hour, Halifax saw a Darryn Stamp header hooked off the line by Donnelly, a Killeen shot blocked by Anthony Straker and a Daryl Taylor shot from distance pushed away by that man Jaimez-Ruiz. At the other end there were decent opportunities for John Grant – against his old club – and Rob Elvins, but it was as if fate had already decreed that no matter what either side created, there would be no goals on this bitterly cold afternoon.

> **"**It was a decent game for a 0-0. We are just pleased to come up here and pick up a point. I was so pleased for the two Ryans and also Mikhael. I wanted to give the lads a run out in the first team and they can feel a part of what has happened this season...
> This was a big game for Halifax, as well as the other teams at the bottom. We wanted to get something out of this game, and we have managed to achieve that.**"**
>
> Gary Waddock

22 April 2008

ALDERSHOT TOWN 0

WEYMOUTH 0

Aldershot football had a ball at the Recreation Ground on Tuesday evening, as the Shots' family came together to celebrate the club's return to the Football League.

That there was a game being played as well was almost a sideshow and it duly failed to live up to the occasion. Still, the 0-0 stalemate left both sides pretty content: a point was enough to secure visitors Weymouth their Blue Square Premier status for next season and also took Aldershot to the outstanding achievement of 100 points for the campaign, still with a game to play, away to Rushden & Diamonds tomorrow.

In a party atmosphere, with close to 6,000 fans squeezed into the Rec, the whole of the East Bank was awash with red and blue – as was Nikki Bull's hair – in keeping with the evening sky as the sun set on Aldershot's time in non-League football. Now there is a new dawn to look forward to of Football League football after Aldershot's triumphant march to the Blue Square Premier title – and with it the big prize of promotion to League Two.

Perhaps the loudest cheers were reserved for half time, when the club paid tribute to the key players – on and off the pitch – who have helped Aldershot football back to where it belongs, in the League, in the 16 years since Aldershot FC's demise and the rebirth in the form of Aldershot Town FC. Players from the old Aldershot FC,

such as striker David Puckett, players who represented both clubs – Colin Fielder and Koo Dumbuya among them – and key members of the board were individually acclaimed by the crowd. Former managers too were warmly received, from Aldershot Town's first manager, Steve Wignall, to Terry Brown.

The reunion was given the perfect toast, with the famous casket of rum, presented to Aldershot Town by Clapton chairman Mike Fogg after their opening game in Diadora League Division Three in August 1992, being opened by Fogg himself and Aldershot's chairman, John McGinty.

Talking of alcohol, a hour or so later, captain Rhys Day duly lifted the Blue Square Premier trophy after the game, to a chorus of cheers and champagne corks popping. Aldershot's trophy cabinet now has two spanking new additions after victory in the Setanta Shield earlier this month. Not bad for an opening season for Gary Waddock as manager.

While Waddock would have loved to have rounded off the home season with a win – there have already been 18 in the league – he was content with a draw, given that it took his side to a magical century of points, which has never been achieved in the Conference.

This was a game that the Shots should have won – John Grant missed a penalty in the first minute of the second half and Weymouth goalkeeper Stephen Henderson

made fine saves from Rob Elvins, Louie Soares and substitute Joel Grant – but Waddock was satisfied.

"We were in control of the game," he said. "We created a lot of chances. On another given day we might have put one of those away and obviously we missed the penalty." Waddock paid tribute to his squad unity, which has played such a key role in all its success. "This season everybody has seen the way the players work for each other. They do have a fantastic team spirit.

> *" From the start we set our stall out and wanted to gain promotion, which we have done. But I have to say, 100 points in a season is quite remarkable. "*

Waddock recalled Soares and Kirk Hudson to the starting line-up and the Shots enjoyed the better of a uninspired first half. The best move saw Ben Harding feed Elvins, who played a slick one-two with John Grant, only to blast his effort straight at Henderson.

Soares, who enjoyed a lively game, ballooned over in all too familiar fashion close to half time, before beating Henderson minutes later, only to see Scott Doe clear his deflected effort off the line.

After the excitement of the half-time interval, the game followed suit, with Doe penalised for a tug on John Grant in the area. But Aldershot's leading scorer hit the right post with his effort from the spot.

"Bully would have scored it," chanted the East Bank, but soon their hero was off the pitch, due to a long-term leg injury. Bull left to rapturous applause; the Rec faithful hope they have not seen the last of the talismanic keeper, who is out of contract in the summer. His replacement, Mikhael Jaimez-Ruiz, made a solid save from Michael Malcolm as Weymouth, who were tidy and organised throughout, pushing for an unlikely win. But the Shots came closest when Henderson denied Joel Grant, after fine play by Lewis Chalmers.

So, normal service at the Rec – a win – was not served up as a season finale. Frankly, who cares, given that the next league fixture at the Rec will be in the Football League.

> *" The dream has come true for us all, players and supporters. "*
>
> Rhys Day

> **What we've achieved is beginning to sink in now, because the trophy is here and we've been presented with it.**
> "We've done a lap of honour in front of our fans, which was quite amazing. It's been just a wonderful, wonderful night.
>
> Tonight was brilliant. It was fantastic of the club to invite everyone back. Everybody has played a part from the day the club was reformed. It's not just about what has happened here tonight, everybody has played their part in some way. It's fantastic."
>
> Gary Waddock

From left to right: John Grant, Rhys Day and Lewis Chalmers.

RUSHDEN & DIAMONDS 1
(Smith 65)

ALDERSHOT TOWN 1
(John Grant 72 pen)

26 April 2008

LINE-UP

Jaimez-Ruiz, Gier, Straker, Charles, Newman (Donnelly 46), Chalmers, Soares, Harding, John Grant, Elvins (Mendes 58), Joel Grant.

Gary Waddock has patiently repeated many a mantra to excitable journalists in post-match interviews this season, successfully deflecting pressure away from his squad as the promotion pressure cooker came to the boil.

But most interviews ended with: "This is a long season, let's just see how many points we end up with at the end of it."

Well, now we and Waddock know: 101. That's a whopping 15 points – five wins – clear of closest rivals Cambridge United and Torquay United.

When Aldershot came to the boil in the race for promotion, Cambridge, Torquay and the like were caught cold. While they were tepid and timid, Waddock's Aldershot were red-hot. And now the chasing pack must enter the cauldron that is the play-offs, while the Shots' players, courtesy of the club, feel the heat of the Mediterranean sun on their backs, basking in an afterglow of champions.

Room 101 may be a place of nightmares in George Orwell's 1984 but, instead, season 2007/08 and its 101 points has been the stuff of dreams for Aldershot and its loyal supporters. They were out in force and fancy-dress to salute their heroes as the sun set on the season at Rushden & Diamonds on Saturday.

Typically of this squad and Waddock, they did not let the fans down, coming from behind to ensure that they remained unbeaten in the league since they were comprehensively outplayed by York City at the end of January, 19 games ago.

Granted, a 1-1 draw was Aldershot's fifth stalemate in the last six league games, but who can blame them for easing off a little when the job was finished well before the completion date.

After the game, Waddock went as far as describing his side's achievements as a 'miracle', before paying tribute to what he regarded as a fitting finale to the season.

> " *It's been an amazing season for me, Martin and the backroom staff. Everybody has played their part.* "
>
> Gary Waddock

"I thought we played really well today, moving the ball around well and creating chances. The pleasing thing is that we have gone a long time now unbeaten. We won the championship a couple of weeks back but we've picked up points since then and haven't lost, which is important."

At times the game was typically end-of-season; after all, the Shots had done their hard work and Rushden, in mid-table, had little to play for. The easy pace and nature of the game certainly suited Ben Harding, who was at his imperious best, making space in midfield and spraying passes with style and substance.

Not for the first time, however, the Shots required a little adversity to reach their peak. After Sam Smith stabbed Rushden ahead in the 65th minute, Aldershot immediately pressed for equality and, after a foul in the area stopped Joel Grant's pacy dribble, John Grant swept home from the spot.

© Mal Swinden / Northants Evening Telegraph

Lewis Chalmers goes close for the Shots in the first half.

Shots make a point and wave goodbye to the Non-League

GARY WADDOCK has patiently repeated many a mantra to excitable journalists in post-match interviews this season, successfully deflecting pressure away from his squad as the promotion pressure-cooker came to the boil.

"We can only concentrate on the next game and the three points on offer," has been the off-the-pitch equivalent of Ben Harding; ever-present.

But most interviews ended with: "This is a long season, let's just see how many points we end up with at the end of it."

Well, now we and Waddock know: 101. That's a whopping 13 points — five wins — clear of closest rivals Cambridge United and Torquay United.

When Aldershot came to the boil in the race for promotion, Cambridge, Torquay and the like were sized and timid, the Ginger Jose's Aldershot sweat-fest. And now the chasing pack most enter the cauldron that is the play-offs, while the Shots' players, courtesy of the club, feel the heat of the Mediterranean sun on their backs, basking in an afterglow of champions.

Room 101 may be a place of nightmares in George Orwell's 1984 but, instead, season 2007-08 and its 101 points has been the stuff of dreams for Aldershot and its loyal supporters. They were out in force and fancy-dress to salute their heroes as the sun set on the season at Rushden & Diamonds on Saturday.

Typically of this squad and Waddock, they did not let the fans down, coming from behind to ensure that they remained unbeaten in the league since they were comprehensively outplayed by York City at the end of January, 19 games ago.

Granted, a 1-1 draw was Aldershot's fifth stalemate in the last six league games, but who can blame them for easing off a little when the job was finished well before the completion date.

After the game, Waddock went as far as describing his side's achievements as a 'miracle', before paying tribute to what he regarded as a fitting finale to the season.

"It's been an amazing season for me. Martin [Kuhl] and the backroom staff. Everybody has played their part," said Waddock.

"The players will have learnt and developed through this season and taken a lot from it. They have grown in confidence from the manner and the way they've played. And the style of it too — and obviously what they've achieved. It's a fantastic season for everybody.

"I thought we played really well today, moving the ball around really well and creating chances. The pleasing thing is that we have gone a long time now unbeaten.

"We won the championship a couple of weeks back but we've picked up points since then and haven't lost, which is important."

At times the game was typically end-of-season; after all, the Shots had done their hard work and Rushden, in mid-table, had little to play for. The easy pace and nature of the game certainly suited Harding, who was at his imperious best, making space in midfield and spraying passes with style and substance.

Not for the first time, however, the Shots required a little adversity to reach their peak. After Sam Smith stabbed Rushden ahead in the 45th minute, Aldershot immediately pressed for equality and, after a foul in the area stopped John Grant's pacy dribble, John Grant swept home from the

minute, the 16th, when Lewis Chalmers had an effort cleared off the line, Harding had a shot saved onto the post by Rushden keeper Martyn Margaroon and John Grant ballooned the rebound over the bar.

Rushden, for whom Dean Howell and Abdou El-Kholti formed an impressive left flank, shaded a lacklustre first half, in which Aldershot had plenty of defending to do, with Ricky Newman and Gier especially solid.

But while Rushden had their moments in the second half — as well as Smith's goal, El Kholti's volley hit a post and Michael Jolmez flair, playing

got sent off at the end of the last day of the season, but things like that happen in football," said Waddock. "But we're not going to be too worried about it. He will miss him at the start of next season but we will just have to adjust accordingly.

Waddock is already busy planning for next season. While the players are on the Costa del Sol before returning for this Sunday's celebrations in Aldershot town centre, Waddock joked that "I might have an hour off come June.

First and foremost, Waddock is waiting for a number of key players to respond to the club's contract offers. The spine of Waddock's midfield and defence

switch off until pre-season but that's not the case. This period now is very busy, as we build towards a new campaign."

Already it is rumoured that Ryan Scott will be leaving the club. The central midfielder's season has been ravaged by injury and the surgery of Chalmers, the big money Scott Donnelly has with little chance of a first future.

And, as far as Waddock is concerned, this season is already history, albeit a hugely historic one. "We'll enjoy this period but we are already looking to the future," said Waddock. "What we've

Rushden & Diamonds 1
Aldershot Town 1

by Charlie Oliver at Nene Park
Blue Square Premier
Match rating: ✗✗✗✗✗
Referee: G Scott
Attd: 2,197

Ben Harding (right) took control of the midfield at Rushden.

The Mail, 29 April 2008.

It was Grant's 20th league goal in a season in which he has been injured twice for a lengthy period. Successfully converting a penalty quickly banished painful memories of his spot-kick miss in last Tuesday's 0-0 draw with Weymouth at the Rec too, even if it did deny Rob Gier the chance to score his first goal for the Shots. Gier attempted to grab the ball after the foul on Joel Grant but the other Grant pulled rank, in rather more amicable fashion than the spat between Chelsea's Didier Drogba and Michael Ballack a few hours previously.

"We went a goal down but that's not the first time that's happened to us this season and we responded," said Waddock. "I'm sure John was a little bit nervous taking the penalty but he slotted it away really well.

> **" As I've said from Day One, it's all about the squad. Every member has played his part. "**

In the first half, Aldershot really only came to life for one minute, the 16th, when Lewis Chalmers had an effort cleared off the line, Harding had a shot saved onto the post by Rushden keeper Martyn Margarson, and John Grant ballooned the rebound over the bar.

Rushden, for whom Dean Howell and Abdou El-Kholti formed an impressive left flank, shaded a lacklustre first half, in which Aldershot had plenty of defending to do, with Ricky Newman and Gier especially solid.

But while Rushden had their moments in the second half – as well as Smith's goal, El-Kholti's volley hit a post and Mikhael Jaimez-Ruiz, playing in place of Nikki Bull who continues to struggle with a leg injury, saved well from Jake Beecroft – Aldershot were the better team, enjoying long periods of concerted pressure.

After a marauding run from Lewis Chalmers had been rudely interrupted, John Grant's flying volley from Harding's curling free kick was just inches wide. Junior Mendes, who was a lively replacement for Rob Elvins, nearly set up Harding for a tap-in and, at the death, Mendes was superbly denied by Margarson, after working space in the area from Joel Grant's clever cutback.

Seconds after that, the game ended on a sour note for Aldershot, when Anthony Straker was given a straight red card for barging substitute Lawrence Lambley to the ground, as he looked to burst clear into the area.

Straker, sent off for two bookings away to Forest Green Rovers in September, is likely to miss the first two matches of the League Two season in August. "Of course I'm disappointed that he [Straker] got sent off at the end of the last day of the season, but things like

that happen in football," said Waddock. "But we're not going to be too worried about it. We will miss him at the start of next season but we will just have to adjust accordingly."

Waddock is already busy planning for next season. First and foremost, he is waiting for a number of key players to respond to the club's contract offers. The spine of the side's midfield and defence – Harding, Chalmers, Anthony Charles and Bull – lead the list of players who have yet to agree terms for next season.

While Harding and Charles look set to stay, rumours persist that Chalmers and Bull may be lured away to a league higher than League Two. Only time will tell.

"We're in the process of sorting out contracts now, over the next week or so," said Waddock. "The players will respond to the offers that have been made. They will return from a thoroughly deserved break away and come back to me and let me know whether they are accepting the offers or not. And then we move on."

Waddock, meticulous to the core, will already have new targets lined up, whether or not key players choose to stay. "We're stepping up a level. Martin and I are extremely positive," said Waddock. "We've got a group of young players and we need to add to that and make the group better.

"Let's see where we are this time next year," he added, in familiar fashion.

> **" What we've achieved now has been put to bed after this game and while the players will enjoy it for a few weeks, when they come back into train they will be focused on a new campaign in League Two. And I'm looking forward to that already. "**
>
> Gary Waddock

ALDERSHOT TOWN FOOTBALL CLUB
Blue Square Premier Champions 2008
"ALIVE AND KICKING"

It's been a brilliant year. I have loved every minute of it. The Torquay game stands out. Winning there, in front of the TV cameras and so many of our fans, was amazing. The celebrations after Exeter were great too – the bus ride home was memorable.

Rob Gier

> " I knew it was a young group and we added to that. Martin and I knew we couldn't be a defensive side as we hadn't got those types of players but, anyway, it would have been going totally against what we wanted to do. "
>
> Gary Waddock

> **"** We are all so grateful to the fans. The older you get, the more you appreciate winning. **"**
>
> Anthony Charles

> **"** The fans played their part – it's not just the players and management. We are all in this together and I can't wait to play in League Two. These are proper supporters and I love them. **"**
>
> John Grant

> " *Gary brought back that camaraderie and the banter between the younger players. There's been a brilliant team spirit this season and the Gaffer has got it just right.* "
>
> Nikki Bull

CONCLUSION

S eason 2007/08 was a dream come true for Aldershot football and its fans: they won promotion back to where they belong, in the Football League.

The rising phoenix that is Aldershot Town has finally emerged from the ashes of Aldershot FC to win back the League status so cruelly lost to the town and its football fans in 1992.

And they did it in style, as Gary Waddock's vibrant young side secured promotion with three games to spare, winning by 15 points, with a record number of points (101) and victories (31) into the bargain.

The simple, wonderful truth is that now, Aldershot Town FC are kicking off season 2008/09 in League Two. The Shots are back among the elite, the 92-strong Football League members.

First up is, appropriately, another club reborn and rebuilt from the embers of a former Football League legend: Accrington Stanley. This is closely followed by a trip in the Carling Cup to Coventry City's Ricoh Arena, a game which will firmly announce the Shots back in the 'big time'.

In a division with a distinctive northern flavour, AFC Bournemouth are the rare southern visitors as Football League action returns to the Recreation Ground – sorry, make that 'The EBB Stadium at the Recreation Ground' – for the first time in more than 16 years.

The name may have changed and a little of the look too, as the club and volunteers worked feverishly across the summer to meet Football League regulations, but to the fans the ground will forever remain 'The Rec', where their football dreams died and were resurrected.

On the pitch, miracle-maker manager Gary Waddock was quick to adjust – or 'tinker' as he put it – his squad over the summer. Ryan Williams and Ryan Scott were released, as was Dean Smith and, more surprisingly, Rob Gier.

In came striker Marvin Morgan from Woking, and defenders Chris Blackburn and Dean Howell from Swindon Town and Rushden & Diamonds respectively. All three have slotted in well during pre-season.

Scott Davies has returned for a season-long loan from Reading, while Ben Starosta, on loan from Sheffield United with a view to a permanent move, has filled Gier's shoes. All of the new players are young, strong and athletic and most of them have a point to prove to former clubs in the Football League. It's the way Waddock and Martin Kuhl want their players to be.

Hence Waddock's delight at tying down to the club all but one of the players he wanted to retain from last season's triumph. Joel Grant was the one who got away, but the loss of his sublime skill was tempered by a club record £130,000 fee from Crewe Alexandra. Otherwise, the side remains, including previously out-of-contract players like the red-blooded and blue-veined Nikki Bull in goal and the midfield maestros Ben Harding and Lewis Chalmers, whose respective southern swagger and northern grit dictated so many matches in Aldershot's favour last season.

But no player will be guaranteed a start in a versatile squad where competition is now fantastically fierce. Waddock has, for instance, five strikers to pick from. And four midfielders who want to play in the middle. All the players are hungry and Waddock must keep them happy too. The manager is never one for public statements of intent but, no doubt, he will have told his squad that, with their fearless football, packed with pace and panache, they can succeed again this season.

Aldershot football certainly returns to the Football League in a better state than it left: the club appears to be on a far more stable footing, the management is assured, the squad is young, talented and confident, and the fans are expected in large numbers.

Their magnificent support was present throughout the non-League adventure too. There were fun and frolics along the way, as the fans stuck by their Shots. That loyalty may have been a blind devotion at the start, but the Shots faithful had a vision – and now it's reality.

Good things come to those who wait, after all. As far as Aldershot Town is concerned, it's the fans who have called the shots. And now they've called the Shots back to the Football League. All together now: "Come on the Shots, come on the Shots…"

Charlie Oliver, August 2008

2007/08 BLUE SQUARE PREMIER LEAGUE TABLE

		Played	Won	Drawn	Lost	For	Against	GD	Points
1	Aldershot Town (C) (P)	46	31	8	7	82	48	34	101
2	Cambridge United	46	25	11	10	68	41	27	86
3	Torquay United	46	26	8	12	83	57	26	86
4	Exeter City (P)	46	22	17	7	83	58	25	83
5	Burton Albion	46	23	12	11	79	56	23	81
6	Stevenage Borough	46	24	7	15	82	55	27	79
7	Histon	46	20	12	14	76	67	9	72
8	Forest Green Rovers	46	19	14	13	76	59	17	71
9	Oxford United	46	20	11	15	56	48	8	71
10	Grays Athletic	46	19	13	14	58	47	11	70
11	Ebbsfleet United	46	19	12	15	65	61	4	69
12	Salisbury City	46	18	14	14	70	60	10	68
13	Kidderminster Harriers	46	19	10	17	71	60	11	67
14	York City	46	17	11	18	71	74	-3	62
15	Crawley Town	46	19	9	18	73	67	6	60
16	Rushden & Diamonds	46	15	14	17	55	55	0	59
17	Woking	46	12	17	17	53	61	-8	53
18	Weymouth	46	11	13	22	53	73	-20	46
19	Northwich Victoria	46	11	11	24	52	78	-26	44
20	Halifax Town (R)	46	12	16	18	61	70	-9	42
21	Altrincham	46	9	14	23	56	82	-26	41
22	Farsley Celtic (R)	46	10	9	27	48	86	-38	39
23	Stafford Rangers (R)	46	5	10	31	42	99	-57	25
24	Droylsden (R)	46	5	9	32	46	103	-57	24

PLAYER STATS

| | 2007-08 SEASON | | | | | |
| | LEAGUE | | CUPS | | TOTAL | |
	APPS	GOALS	APPS	GOALS	APPS	GOALS
Nikki Bull	44	-	8	-	52	-
Lewis Chalmers	41 + 1	3	8 + 2	-	49 + 3	3
Anthony Charles	35	1	5 + 3	1	40 + 3	2
Scott Davies	24 + 5	10	11 + 2	1	35 + 7	11
Rhys Day	32 + 4	3	9 + 2	2	41 + 6	5
Scott Donnelly	2 + 6	1	7 + 1	4	9 + 7	5
Rob Elvins	29 + 8	7	10 + 2	4	39 + 10	11
Rob Gier	38	-	7 + 1	-	45 + 1	-
Joel Grant	20 + 10	4	9 + 3	2	29 + 13	6
John Grant	32 + 2	20	5 + 3	5	37 + 5	25
Ben Harding	46	5	9 + 1	1	55 + 1	6
George Hardy	-	-	2 + 1	-	2 + 1	-
Kirk Hudson	18 + 17	7	7 + 6	8	25 + 23	15
Josh Huggins	-	-	0 + 3	-	0 + 3	-
Danny Hylton	9 + 14	5	9 + 5	1	18 + 19	6
Mikhael Jaimez Ruiz	2 + 1	-	9	-	11 + 1	-
Miles Jones	-	-	1	1	1	1
Junior Mendes	3 + 3	1	3 + 1	3	6 + 4	4
Jason Milletti	-	-	5	-	5	-
Ricky Newman	14 + 13	2	10	-	24 + 13	2
Lewis Phillips	-	-	1	1	1	1
Dan Read	-	-	0 + 1	-	0 + 1	-
Emmanuel Sackey	-	-	1 + 2	-	1 + 2	-
Ryan Scott	1	-	0 + 2	-	1 + 2	-
Daniel Simmonds	0 + 1	-	1	-	1 + 1	-
Dean Smith	6 + 2	-	9 + 2	-	15 + 4	-
Louie Soares	30 + 7	4	12 + 2	3	42 + 9	7
Anthony Straker	43	-	12 + 1	1	55 + 1	1
Ryan Williams	1	-	-	-	1	-
Dave Winfield	18 + 6	1	9	1	27 + 6	2

FAN PAGE

Neil & Ryan Atherton
Ian Barnett
Robin Allan Best
Bob Bowden
Dave Brewer
William Kenny Brown
Charles Bryant
David Buckley
Steve 'Chappie' Chapman
Andrew Chillman
John Clark
Alan Clarkson
Paul Coates
Tim, Jude & Louis Cowden
Christopher Davies
R. Dowding
Pip, Ella & Tash Duff
Sarah Elcombe
Barry Elliott
Daniel, Zachary & Malachy Evans
Simon Evans
Tony Excell
Rod Farr
Colin Figg
!FLAGBOY!
Richard & Jack Ford
Matthew Franklin
Steven Gibbs
Martin Goddard
Norman John Gray
James Greenwood
John Hannah
Barry Harcourt
Terry Harper
Martin Harrington
Alex Hickey
Terry Hillyer
Mark Holt
Dennis Hoppe
John Horlock
Lesley Hubbard
Emily & Lucy Hunt
Michael Jones
Chris Kane

Liam Kane
Peter Kersley
Christy Kuplic
Mr Michael J. Lord
Mr Kenneth Lovegrove
Cath & Chris Lyons
Daniel Marsh
Craig Matthews
Mac McKenna
Brian Meeres
Graham Oliver
Harriet Oliver
William Oliver
Chris Osborne
Barry Ruffle
Daniel & Thomas Parmiter
Jon Potterton
David Price
S. Shelley
Nigel Shirley
Alton Shot
Dulas Shot (Pete Bradley)
Shetland Shot (Andy Bradley)
Barry Smith
Carl Smith
Jeremy Smith
Robert Smith
Sue Smith
Pete Stanford
Simon Stevens
Lauren Storey
Bill Taylor
Trevor Taylor
Mark Treadwell
Arthur John Varney
Sam Viggers
Graham Whapshott
Gary Whapshott
Sian Williams
Trevor Wisker
www.strayshots.co.uk
The Wythe Family
Phil Yarney
Robert Young